MW00810292

Women, Gender, and the West

Renee M. Laegreid, general editor

Divinely Guided: The California Work of the Women's National Indian Association, by Valerie Sherer Mathes

Their Lives, Their Wills: Women in the Borderlands, 1750–1846, by Amy M. Porter

What Is Gone

Amy Knox Brown

Foreword by Lorraine Lopez

Texas Tech University Press

This book is typeset in Minion Pro. The paper used in this book meets the minimum requirements of ANSI/NISO Z39.48-1992 (R1997). ∞

Designed by Kasey McBeath

Library of Congress Cataloging-in-Publication Data
[CIP TK]

17 18 19 20 21 22 23 24 25 / 9 8 7 6 5 4 3 2 1

Texas Tech University Press
Box 41037 | Lubbock, Texas 79409-1037 USA
800.832.4042 | ttup@ttu.edu | www.ttupress.org

For BAK

Contents

Foreword

I was just five or six, the second-born of four sisters. When our mother couldn't bring all of us along on an errand, she would leave my older sister and me in the care of my father's sister and her husband. These were the only relatives to relocate with my parents from New Mexico to California in the 1950s, so they were our go-to extended family, ubiquitous on holidays and often present for Sunday dinners. Warm, sharp, and generous, my childless aunt was a gifted storyteller with a terrific sense of humor. To the bafflement of my housekeeping-averse mother, my aunt relished cleaning. As she bustled about scrubbing and sweeping, she would sound her triumphal battle cry: ¡Sucio! Filth—it was in every nook and cranny to challenge and thrill her. My aunt could not have borne it if my uncle were slovenly, and he was not. Despite being an itinerant housepainter, he dressed impeccably in wide-lapelled pinstriped suits on Sundays and holidays, and he wore starched and pressed khakis on workdays. Yet, my aunt called him *sucio*, too, but in a low, bitter voice.

An asthmatic, my uncle breathed noisily and huffed often on his inhaler. His breathing grew even more ragged when he watched over my older sister and me while my aunt, a practical nurse, was working. He would hold us on his lap, one at a time. He patted and petted us, squeezed our thighs. His thick-fingered hands wandered and probed. This felt strange, but warm and tingly, and then the ticklish feeling grew persistent and painful. I'd wrench away to slam into the bathroom, where I'd perch on the closed toilet seat, trembling. Before long, my sister's knuckles would peck against the door, and I'd crack it open to let her in. We would then wait together in that cramped bathroom, often eyeing the razor strap and the mauve oval-shaped soap-on-a-rope that hung on the towel rack. I'd fantasize about using these if he burst in. But he never did. We'd strain our ears listening to the ticking silence, followed by our uncle's heavy footsteps. At last, the television would snap on, and the apartment vibrated with syncopated sounds. We'd inhale, aware with that first dizzying gulp that we'd been holding our breath while the floorboards groaned under his feet.

We never told our parents about our uncle, what he did to us. My sister and I were ashamed of our tacit complicity, our failure to protect one another and ourselves. Accustomed to praise for being good girls, for doing what we were told, we would go to our uncle when he called us to sit on his lap. How could we disobey an adult? How could we say no to our uncle? And perhaps, too, we sensed that if we spoke of what he did to us, we would wound our beloved aunt, jeopardizing our connection to her. Moreover, we didn't speak about this because we had no idea how to talk about it. Unlike children of today, we lacked words to describe what our uncle had done. We'd never heard of good and bad touching, let alone molestation. We had no language even to discuss this with one another. Instead, we learned polite disobedience: how to edge away, smiling but shaking our heads when our uncle beckoned us; how to refuse when he'd ask if we wanted to see his "birdie"; and even how to pry our younger sister, a toddler then, out of his lap, when she was left with us in his care. Before long, our mother began hiring a family friend's daughter to babysit us, and we no longer spent time alone with our uncle.

Until we were young women, we remained unable to name what had happened to us. And then, when we finally talked about it, we agreed that we were lucky to have had each other. The experience, in fact, forged a bond between us, one that precluded sibling rivalry, even squabbling, and one that has lasted to this day. Compared to the violence suffered by many, we were indeed very lucky—my sister and I—that this was the only form of sexual abuse we have endured. It's strange now to look back at that time, to glimpse those two little girls shuddering in a bathroom, and think of them as lucky. To consider this a narrative of luck.

Our uncle molested, but did not rape us, and that was lucky. When our parents began leaving our younger sister with him, we protected her—more luck! According to the Department of Justice and Centers for Disease Control and Prevention, one in six women has experienced attempted or completed rape, so the fact that both of us grew into middle age without again enduring sexual assault seems a clear karmic blessing. But what a baseline for good fortune. Yet even a bar as low as this plummets further for rape victims who often construe themselves to be lucky to survive their attacks and luckier still in the rare cases when their assailants are caught and successfully prosecuted. Victims of sexual assault endure intimate violation, acts that threaten to dehumanize and dismantle belief systems on which identity is built. Perhaps a luck narrative is the first step toward reclaiming that unique and exceptional entity: the self.

Inspired by Alice Sebold's *Lucky*, Amy Knox Brown's memoir likewise inscribes her brutal rape and its punishing aftermath. But while Sebold's title alludes to the cruel irony of a first-responder's careless comment, Brown restructures and challenges the viewpoint supporting such an utterance, claiming it as one she held prior to her assault. She maps this retelling over various time periods and between two specific locations in Nebraska: Omaha, where she was raped; and Lincoln, where she grew up and lived as a young woman when Candice Harms, a student at the University of Nebraska, vanished. In this way, the memoir weaves together autobiographic, geographic, and temporal strands that cohere, accruing meaning even as they deconstruct the author's personal experience narrative of middle-class privilege and exceptionalism—a charmed life spent in safe spaces.

What ensues is a dynamic contemplation of self and place in Omaha and Lincoln, Nebraska, filtered through the experience of sexual violence. The braided narrative builds suspense, replicating for readers the author's prolonged periods of not knowing as the events of her rape, its aftermath, and the disappearance of Candice Harms play out. From the first page, readers are in the hands of a gifted writer, one adept at re-creating experience through sensory detail. Such details—the apple she munches as she walks alone on the night she is attacked, the campaign buttons (I Like Ike) that spill out of her purse, the mud on the ground, and the moon "like an object caught in a spider's web"—resonate metaphorically to foreshadow and simulate events in a way that is unforgettable, even harrowing.

Further, the memoir's layered reflections on self and location assert the inextricable connection between identity and place. Narrating sexual violence becomes a way to articulate the presence of absence suggested by the title, *What Is*

Gone. As such, Brown inventories features—stores, restaurants, bars, neighborhoods—of her native city (Lincoln) as they transform or vanish much in the way that her uncomplicated understanding of who she is ("a lucky girl") and where she is from ("a safe place") alters in the aftermath of rape. The writing tracks this epistemological shift, wherein the author interrogates her knowledge of self and place and how such knowledge is obtained. Brown provides an apt metaphor for this transformation by referencing a long-held belief, conferred by her father's insistence that the Lincoln capitol building is one of the Seven Wonders of the World. Despite contradictory evidence, the author perpetuates her father's claim, as errant as her own insistence on middle-class exceptionalism.

When she later beholds superior architectural designs while living in Washington, D.C., Brown must at last surrender the belief that she had shared with her father. Similarly, the experience of rape and the disappearance of Candice Harms bring pressure to bear on her ideas of self and place, ultimately producing a new and paradoxical understanding: (1) She is a lucky/unlucky girl, and (2) Lincoln is a safe place/Lincoln is not a safe place. In embracing irreconcilable truths, Brown invokes F. Scott Fitzgerald's observation: "The test of a first-rate intelligence is the ability to hold two opposed ideas in mind at the same time and still retain the ability to function." This offers an epiphany for Brown. Her undertaking in articulating her experience and this recognition usher her toward a higher order of thinking and functioning. As a consequence, her work in this memoir provides survivors of sexual assault a narrative from which to draw wisdom and strength, a way to make sense of what is senseless.

My sister, now a social worker who often deals with traumatized clients, observes that when people can put words to their experiences, they begin to separate from suffering as they struggle to organize and control it through narration. As a writer, I know firsthand that expressing in words that which terrifies me is the most effective way to overcome fear. As a reader, I've found that absorbing experiences of others on the page provides the means of communication that can be crucial for articulating one's own trauma, as well as the ideation to illuminate the dark corners of memory, to flush monsters from the shadows and sweep these—as my aunt would when taking the broom to her kitchen floor—into the dustbin. Though in no way as easy as that, Amy Knox Brown's *What Is Gone* captures and contextualizes sexual violence, forging bonds with readers and providing terms of discourse and inspiration for others likewise to author their own narratives.

Lorraine Lopez
Vanderbilt University, Nashville, Tennessee

Acknowledgments

For information surrounding the trial of Joe N. Griffin, I consulted articles published in the *Omaha World Herald*. Information regarding the Candice Harms case was obtained from articles in the *Lincoln Journal Star* and an interview with Tom Casady. I also consulted the *Lincoln Journal* regarding the Jane Weaver case.

This book began as an essay written during the 2010 University of Nebraska-Lincoln's Summer Writers Conference class taught by Meghan Daum. The essay was published in the Fall 2011 issue of *Virginia Quarterly Review*. Salem College provided research support during the writing of the book manuscript.

Thanks to early readers of the manuscript for their support and sound advice: Karen Palmer, Aimee Mepham, John McNally, and especially Tekla Johnson. Editor Judith Keeling combines the skill of Maxwell Perkins with the patience of a saint. This book would not exist in its present form without her wise counsel.

What Is Gone

Chapter 1 :: **Omaha, 1985**

On Wednesday, February 20, I stepped out of the Midtown apartment I shared with my best friend, Abby, and three other girls. It was a little after ten o'clock, and the night air felt oddly and pleasantly warm for this time of year. In fact, the past few days had been temperate enough to melt all the winter snow, and now the air held the damp scent of approaching spring. Shutting the door behind me, I gave it a little tug to make sure the lock had engaged, then went down the steps that led to Farnam Street. I was heading to my boyfriend Jim's condo, which was less than a block away as a crow flies. I hadn't bothered with a coat; I was warm enough in one of my favorite shirts, a burgundy flannel with a navy Ralph Lauren polo player stitched on the chest. I looked to my right before stepping off the curb—Farnam was a one-way street—and bit into the apple I'd brought with me.

I didn't bother glancing to the left, where a bar called Jasper's stood two doors down, because no traffic would be approaching from that direction. If I'd looked, I might have seen the man standing outside Jasper's.

I was twenty-three years old, and I considered myself a lucky person, exempt from the difficulties and tragedies that plagued other people. My life was following the pattern you saw in romantic comedies. In the way that more adventurous people move to New York after college, I was spending a year in Omaha, the big city an hour northeast of Lincoln, where I'd grown up. I was on my own and dating a boy in medical school.

Ever since second grade, when I first knew I wanted to write, I'd practiced narrating to myself what I was doing or thinking. On this particular evening, I thought: *Eating an apple, she crosses Farnam Street, conscious of the strangely warm air. The wet ground smells of mud. She's on her way to see her boyfriend, a second-year med student. From him, she's learned words like clavicle and beta-blocker. She takes the shortcut behind Convenient Food Mart. Bits of gravel crunch under her topsiders.*

Behind Convenient Food Mart was a parking lot that I crossed in the direction of Jim's condo. I heard someone behind me call out, "Hey."

I turned.

A man stood under the streetlight behind the Food Mart. My brain registered details: black, tall, wearing a coat and hat. A scarf hung around his neck. Older than I was, probably in his late twenties or early thirties. "Can I talk to you for a minute?" he asked.

A nudge of instinct whispered, *Run.* I was, after all, only a short distance—fifty yards or so—from my boyfriend's. But what if the man was harmless, merely some guy behind Convenient Food Mart? I'd look paranoid, rude, racist. I was particularly conscious that running would make me look like a racist. Instead, I said, "No." I picked up my pace. I'd almost reached the edge of the lot when an arm jerked tight around my neck. The blade of a knife glinted on the right side of my face.

He'd moved so quietly I hadn't heard him approach.

I tried to scream. He tightened his grip and lifted my feet off the ground. I dropped the apple; the police would find it later when they came to photograph the scene. By then, the fruit's flesh had turned brown where I'd bitten into it.

The man dragged me across the grassy lot that abutted the condo's lawn. I lost my footing and fell. He crouched over me and held his hand hard against my throat. He wanted money. I pulled out the bills I had in my pocket, a five and a one. "That all you got?" He sounded angry. "That all?"

I turned my purse upside down and shook out everything inside it: gum wrappers, two I Like Ike buttons that belonged to my mother, a comb. A few pennies clinked together on the ground. I opened the wallet to show him it was empty.

He shook his head in disgust.

I felt myself slide into a mental state where rationality and craziness collided. That is, I was willing to entertain any idea that would let me stand up and get away from him, no matter how ridiculous. "Look," I said, "we can go to Hinky Dinky and I'll write out a check." That's what I always did when I needed cash: wrote out a check at Hinky Dinky's customer service desk. The store was about six blocks away, and I imagined all the opportunities I might have for escape. I could run in front of a car, screaming for help, or duck into a store as we passed, or—if we made it all the way to Hinky Dinky—I'd fill in the memo section of the check with a plea for help. *Call the police*, I'd write. *This man is robbing me.*

An alley ran along the south side of the lot, and I heard a car's tires rumbling over the asphalt. The man held the knife in front of my face and pressed his hand hard against my windpipe. He said, "You better not fuck with me, bitch."

Why didn't the driver look over?

The car paused at the end of the alley and then turned onto 38th Avenue and headed toward Dodge, the busy street one block north.

The man jerked me to my feet. He wedged his arm under my chin and half-carried, half-dragged me across the lot and toward the street.

Why didn't a car appear? Why didn't someone leave one of the houses that faced 38th Avenue right at that moment? But all the houses were dark. Everyone—mostly students, this close to the med center—was probably asleep, or out.

I couldn't scream—the man was carrying me with my feet barely touching the ground, with his arm pressed hard against my throat—but in my head I was shouting to Jim: *Come outside!*

On the east side of 38th Avenue, the man dragged me behind a garage. An old garage with peeling paint, accordion doors. Dark, secluded, though I heard traffic over on Dodge Street, the quick swish of cars as they passed the intersection.

Why didn't anyone turn onto 38th Avenue?

I wheezed and gagged as I tried to breathe and my brain screamed at me to do something, to get some air. He loosened his chokehold and pushed me backwards onto the ground. The dampness of mud seeped through my shirt. "Please don't kill me," I said.

He said he wouldn't, if I did what he wanted. "Take off your jeans."

I said that if he was going to rape me, I wasn't going to help him by removing my clothes.

He held the knife in front of my face. "Do it," he said.

I undid the button at the waistband. I slid the zipper's teeth down their track. My hands shook. I hooked my thumbs inside my underwear and pushed them and my jeans down to my knees.

A full moon hung in the sky. He tried to kiss me. I smelled alcohol on his breath, the odor of unwashed clothes. The rational part of my mind catalogued details of his appearance: wire-rimmed glasses, dark green stocking cap, stubble on his face. Canvas-like pants, not jeans. A canvas-like coat. I felt the scarf's fringe against my bare legs and made note that it was a knitted scarf, not a fabric one.

How could I get away from him? He'd said he wouldn't kill me, but I wasn't sure I believed him. I was crying, but trying to stifle the sound be-cause I could tell it irritated him—*Shut up that noise*—and looking at the full moon, which shone through the bare branches of a tree, so that the planetoid appeared like an object caught in a spider's web. I thought: *What if the full moon is the last thing I ever see?*

And it occurred to me what a cliché that was, my own thoughts at what might be the end of my life. I didn't like this understanding that I gained, that I was a clichéd thinker, not as smart and unusual as I believed, and absolutely not a lucky girl.

He was flaccid. He made sure I knew he still had the knife in his hand, and he pushed my head between his legs.

In *The World According to Garp*, I remembered, a woman accidentally bites off her lover's penis when the car they're in is rear-ended. Could I do that now, intentionally?

If I tried, and it didn't work, he would definitely kill me, I thought. But

I had another, better idea. My jeans were at my knees, cuffing my legs together; I knew I wouldn't be able to run unless I removed them. "It'll work better if I take these off," I said. How calm I sounded.

He nodded.

I slid off my shoes. I pushed my jeans over my knees, down my shins, and left them in a heap to one side.

Did my sudden cooperativeness strike him as strange? Or did he think I was coming around, beginning to see the act as consensual rather than forced?

"Let me get on top," I said.

He lay on his back.

I moved so that I was crouching, as if preparing to follow through on my suggestion, but when I began to stand, he realized what I was doing. He lunged into a sitting position and grabbed the front of my shirt.

I should've taken off my shirt. Then I would've gotten away.

"Don't fuck with me, bitch," he said. "Don't fuck with me." He was still holding the knife. He shoved me against the ground and managed to force himself inside me. I stared at the sky. The air in the shadows of the garage was colder than the air had felt when I left the apartment. I tried to keep absolutely still, no wincing or gagging. After he'd ejaculated, he stood. "Your pants are over there," he said and pointed to where I'd left my jeans.

The back of my shirt was soaked through, mud cold and slimy against my legs. I sat up.

"I saw you," he said, conversationally, "when you came out of your house. I was outside that bar on 40th Street."

"Jasper's?" I asked. I reached for my jeans.

"Yeah," he said. "Jasper's."

Abby and I had gone to Jasper's a couple of weeks earlier, on a Saturday night, with Jim and some of his friends. That night had been cold. I remembered frost blooming in the corners of the bar's windows and candles in red glass containers burning on the tables.

If only I'd looked that direction, too, before crossing the street. If I'd seen him, I'd have gone back inside, told Abby, "There's some weird guy lurking outside Jasper's," and called Jim to come get me.

Jasper's was a good clue, I thought. I could hand it over to the police, and they'd be impressed at how well I'd done, getting information.

He finished zipping his pants. I sat on the ground, jeans bunched in my hands. I felt my molars knocking together. Muscles in my back and legs twitched. He tugged at the sides of his coat. Then, without another word, he pivoted and ducked around the side of the garage. His footsteps receded. He sounded like he was running, and going straight east, not cutting over to Dodge Street. I stood up and looked to make sure he was gone— yes, he really was gone—and then, holding my muddy jeans against my chest, my underwear wadded inside them, I ran across the street to Jim's condo.

•

At the hospital, the nurse was calm and quiet. I stood on a sheet of paper while she ran a tool under my fingernails to collect evidence and combed through my pubic hair to see if any of his hairs had been left behind. The doctor who performed the pelvic exam kept apologizing. "I'm sorry if this hurts," he said, over and over. I stared at the ceiling. The nurse held my hand. She stroked my hair whenever I flinched.

After the medical work was done, I talked to the police, who had arrived at the hospital. They took a statement and photographed my bruised throat. My clothes—that favorite Ralph Lauren shirt and my Calvin Klein jeans and my mud-soaked underwear—were sealed in a plastic bag and taken off to a laboratory for testing.

Everyone, as I remember, was very professional and kind. I was praised, over and over, for not showering, for coming to the hospital right away, for talking to the police and for giving them such a complete description of the suspect. No one said, "What possessed you to walk down an alley at 10 o'clock at night?" No one gave me a look that called my judgment into question. No one, in short, engaged in any sort of blaming the victim. While I didn't exactly blame myself for what happened, and I believed I should be able to walk anywhere I wanted, at any time I wanted, when I said the words, "Walking down the alley," I thought: *Stupid. You sound like a stupid, reckless girl.*

Or an innocent one. Like a person who grew up in Lincoln, Nebraska, and jogged down Sheridan Boulevard at three in the morning when she was in high school and couldn't sleep, and believed herself to be perfectly, eternally safe.

Chapter 2 :: Lincoln, 1960s

I read somewhere that nostalgia is a form of sentimentality.

I also read Ernest Hemingway's advice about writing: "The writer's job is to tell the truth. All you have to do is write one true sentence. Write the truest sentence that you know . . . and then go on from there. . . . There was always one true sentence that I knew or had seen or had heard someone say."

Here's a true sentence: When I was eight years old, my father told me that the Nebraska state capitol building was one of the Seven Wonders of the World.

The trouble with nostalgia is that it leads to oversimplification. I could say that growing up, I loved stories and I loved my hometown. Of course that's reductive, abstract. Let me, instead, pick a particular year and tell you what it was like.

In 1966, our family is living on South 26th Street in Lincoln, Nebraska. What is happening in the larger world? John Lennon sparks outrage when he states in an interview that the Beatles are more popular than Jesus. The last Studebaker factory is closed. President Lyndon Johnson signs the Uniform Time Act, which standardizes the application of Daylight Savings Time. Across the United States, demonstrators protest the Vietnam War. Ronald Reagan is elected governor of California. NOW (the National Organization of Women) is founded. The Reverend Dr. Martin Luther King Jr. leads a civil rights march in Chicago. In *Miranda v. Arizona*, the Supreme Court holds that police must inform suspects of their rights before questioning them.

We move in closer: In February 1966, the Beat poet Allen Ginsberg travels through Lincoln. He writes a poem describing this occasion. His poem refers to the main thoroughfare through town, O Street, as Zero Street.

I won't know of Ginsberg's poem until much later, when I'm in graduate school, because in 1966, I'm four years old and the world as I know it centers around grocery shopping and department stores.

Our house is conveniently located within a mile of four grocery stores, with Ideal Grocery three blocks away on 27th Street; and Binger's, Hinky Dinky, and Safeway situated in a line from 25th to 27th on O Street. Every Wednesday night, Mother examines the flyers in the newspaper and makes her grocery list, which consists of the loss leaders from each of the four stores, along with a few necessary staples. She never buys anything unless it is on sale, and she never deviates from the list.

We devote Thursday mornings from nine a.m. until noon to grocery shopping. For years, I will assume this is how everyone shops for food, but when I describe the procedure to a friend in high school, she looks at me with shock. "We'd go to one place," she says, "and get what we wanted."

First we drive to Binger's, then to Hinky Dinky, then to Safeway. Our last stop is Ideal Grocery, the store closest to home. Ideal is a *nice* store, on the expensive side, with meat cut fresh to order and a man in the produce department who helps you select your fruit and vegetables. You tuck them in a brown paper sack, which he takes to his scale, weighs, and then marks the price with a black crayon on the outside of the bag. Ideal has peculiar, old-fashioned shopping carts that consist of a sturdy metal frame that holds two baskets, one above the other. The cashiers are men in their twenties who've worked in the store since they were teenagers. My favorite cashiers are a pair of twins who remind me of the Smothers Brothers, one taller and blond, the other shorter and dark haired. They always greet us by name. I'd taken one of my dolls along on an earlier trip, and today the dark-haired twin asks, "Where's Susie Marilyn this morning?"

"At home," I say. "She's sleeping."

•

In 1966, and for many years afterwards, Hovland Swanson occupies the storefront west of the NBC Bank Building on the corner of 13th and O in downtown Lincoln. The sidewalk in front of Hovland's had been treated with something that makes it give off glitters of light when the sun hits. I am fascinated by the sidewalk—it seems like something out of a fairy tale, almost too luxurious to actually walk on—and puzzled. What are the glitters made of? They appear to be on the surface of the asphalt, like dropped dimes, but are attached so firmly that you can't dislodge them by scraping the heel of your shoe hard against a particular glitter.

Hovland's isn't exactly a department store. They don't carry furniture and notions and records, like Miller and Paine, which is kitty-corner across O Street. Hovland's stocks clothes, shoes, and gifts. Glass cabinets filled with jewelry and cosmetics line the main floor. Silky scarves hang from racks. The shoe department's walls are blue-green, a color that co-ordinates with the upholstery on chairs set around the room. A salesman named Dick works in the shoe department. My mother knows him from working at Hovland's before she was married. When we go to Hovland's, we always check to see if Dick is there. If he is, Dick and my mother hold elliptical conversations I find boring: *Is she still here?* My mother asks.

Where else would she be? Dick replies.

Mother shakes her head. *Some people.*

You can say that again.

Hovland's sponsors fashion shows, using local girls as the models. In the spring of 1966, I'm included in the Easter fashion show.

I model a dress that is fancier and more expensive than anything my mother would buy, made of navy and white plaid fabric with a red sash around the waist. I wear a straw hat anchored in place by an elastic band stretched under my chin. The shoes are white, patent leather Mary Janes— beautiful, and also fancier than anything I own. They're too big for my feet, so the toes have been stuffed with tissue paper, and I have to concentrate extra hard to walk without tripping. The clerk in charge of the models gives me a little stuffed rabbit to hold. I secretly hope I'll be permitted to keep the rabbit, which strikes me as the best part of the whole wonderful outfit.

The model training is fairly perfunctory. Moments before I walk onto the stage, a T-shaped raised surface surrounded by chairs, the clerk crouches down and says, "See that stage?"

I nod.

"You walk down to the end, and then walk to the little part on the right. Do you know which side is right?"

I point.

"That's good. When you get to the end of the right-side part, turn all the way around so we can see the back of the dress, and then turn around again at the left-side part. And then walk back to me. Can you do that?"

"Yes," I say.

After the girl ahead of me returns, I step out onto the runway. It's difficult to walk in the too-big shoes, so I move slowly, clutching the rabbit against my chest. Bright lights shine down on the stage. I look for my mother in the audience but can't see her. I hear someone whisper, "How darling!"

At the end of the runway, I go to the right, forget to complete a full turn, head for the left side, where I do remember to turn, and walk carefully back down the long part of the T.

The elastic band of the hat digs into my skin. I lift and lower my tissue-stuffed shoes. The dress's price tag has been tucked inside the sleeve, and the little cardboard square pokes against my arm. When I arrive at the starting point, the next girl starts down the runway. The clerk gently removes the rabbit from my hand. She sets it on a shelf with a stuffed chick and a basket of Easter eggs I'd seen one of the other girls carrying. She pats my straw hat and says, "You did a good job."

She directs another clerk to help me change out of my modeling dress. I cast a last look at the stuffed rabbit, then follow the clerk to find my normal clothes: a skirt and blouse my mother had sewn out of fabric we'd bought across the street at Miller and Paine, white ankle socks, also from Miller's, and the ugly saddle shoes, whose heels were scuffed from an attempt to pry the glitters out of the sidewalk in front of Hovland's.

•

I would say that my childhood was one brushed with moments of modest luxury. That is, my family was firmly situated in the middle class—well, maybe not entirely, given the penny-pinching quality of my mother's grocery shopping habits—but there were opportunities for touching the luxury that was contained in Hovland Swanson. We enjoyed the comfort and security that come from knowing the people who worked in the stores, of feeling welcomed, of feeling known.

The comforting sense of predictability shifted, however, once I started school. We'd moved into the house on 26th Street when I was a year old and lived there until shortly before I turned eight. I started school at Elliott Elementary, which was about half a mile away.

My best friend Dallas lived across the street. She was five years older than me. Dallas and I walked to school together, but then went our separate ways, since her classes were in a different part of the building. My school friends were Daphne and Maria.

I was the sort of obedient, task-oriented student that teachers liked, and I enjoyed most parts of school: it was like a job you went to, a duty that gave shape to the day. Reading lessons could be dull—I already knew how to read, having been taught by Dallas's older sisters Marlene and Shirley when I was four—and so I sat quietly after deciphering the words the teacher had revealed on the large tablet resting on an easel, and waited and waited for poor Dickie to sound out *Spot* or *Mother* so we could move on to the next page. I liked the assignments involving storybook paper (lined on the bottom for writing, blank on the top for illustrations) and the yearly fundraiser run by the PTA called Fun Night, where you could win candy and toys.

Recess could go either way, good or bad. Jumping rope or playing games with the girls was fun. Other times, a pack of boys in our class would gang up on someone—a girl or a weaker boy—taunting and shoving until the victim cried. The rest of us learned quickly enough the futility of going to the rescue, because the mean boys would turn on you, too. So while the boys toyed with their victim, the rest of us stood by, helpless, wishing that a teacher would come outside and notice, or that the principal would look out his office window, storm onto the playground, and put an end to the torment.

There were four or five mean boys. The ringleaders were Russell Fowler and Hobart Bradley. The two of them had a little code that they'd use to warn their victim that her number was up: holding index and middle fingers in a V-shape, Russell or Hobart would draw his fingertips from his eyes down his cheeks to indicate falling tears. This part of the gesture meant that someone was going to cry.

The next part of the gesture consisted of a fist tapped twice into the opposite palm: someone was going to cry because she was going to get beat up.

For the third, and final, part of the threat, Russell or Hobart would unclench his fist, extend his index finger, and jab it once, dramatically, at the intended victim. So the entire code spelled out, went like this: someone is going to cry because she'll be beaten up, and that person is *you*.

They'd make the gesture before recess, or near the end of the school day if they planned to follow someone home and beat her up on the way.

Why didn't we tell?

I don't know. We must have thought that the threats and shoves existed purely in the world of children, that they were something we had to deal with ourselves; or that they were simply another part of school, like reading and math, a lesson to be learned. And a tremendous stigma was attached to *telling*. It was more honorable to be a victim than a snitch.

•

One fall day at after-lunch recess, the other girls and I played tag. No one had gotten the tears-punch-punch-you signal that day, so we didn't pay any attention to the mean boys, who loitered under the jungle gym.

Maria was It. She chased after me, and I ran toward the middle of the playground to get away. We were both laughing. The other girls were shouting for me to run faster, for Maria to catch me.

Suddenly, the pack of mean boys infiltrated our game. A couple of them surrounded Maria like a fence. Hobart and Russell and short, red-headed Dickie—who couldn't learn to read and smelled of unwashed laundry—came after me. I ran toward the school building, but they cut me off. Hobart grabbed my arm. My feet slid on the gravel and I fell.

Dickie crouched behind my head and held my shoulders. I kicked and thrashed, yelling to let me go. But what good was yelling in the middle of recess when everyone else was yelling, too?

Hobart took hold of my ankle, his fingers digging into my sock. I kicked at him with my free leg, and he laughed, then closed his other hand on my kicking foot. I tried to pull free, and his fingers tightened.

I had no idea what might happen. I said, "Stop it!" Gravel pressed into my shoulders. Somebody was screaming over by the tetherball pole. Then Russell Fowler reached between my legs. He deliberately ran his fingers along the seam of my pants. I struggled to push him away.

"I got her!" he yelled. "I got her thing."

Apparently that had been the boys' goal, their own version of tag: to pin down one of the girls and touch her, because after they'd done that, they let go of my arms and legs. I stood up. I brushed off my pants. I was conscious of the fact that the humiliation attached to this incident felt worse, more personal, more internal, than the humiliation of being shoved or tripped. Walking away, the boys looked over their shoulders and made the sort of faces that said, *We got you. We got you good.*

Maria approached. "Are you okay?" she asked.

My palms were abraded from the gravel. "I need to wash my hands," I said. Someone somewhere blew a whistle, and recess was over.

That afternoon when I got home, I told my mother what had happened. She called the school, and said that the next day I'd need to talk to the assistant principal about what the boys had done.

Talking to the assistant principal, I thought, would only make things worse. I didn't know what could be done to make them stop; the whole group couldn't be expelled for the rest of their lives, and even if they were expelled, they'd lurk outside Elliott and torment the law-abiding students after school let out. I couldn't imagine any scenario that wouldn't result in retribution *from* the boys for being a tattletale.

Clearly my mother had more faith in the system. I had to talk to Mr. Fletcher, she insisted. Something had to be done about those boys' behavior.

The following day, before recess, Mr. Fletcher walked into our classroom and said something to the teacher, who looked at me and beckoned *Come here.*

I felt the other students watching as I followed Mr. Fletcher out the door and down the hallway to his office. He was scarily tall—taller than the main principal—but had a soft, accented voice. My mother had said that Mr. Fletcher was from Jamaica.

In his office, Mr. Fletcher perched on a corner of his desk. I sat in a chair, facing him. He said to tell him what had happened yesterday on the playground.

Recess had started. Everyone else was outside. I wondered if my class-mates thought I was in the principal's office getting punished for some infraction, but I was the sort of girl who never got in trouble.

I knew if I told on Russell and Hobart, and they found out, they'd beat me up. I said that yesterday on the playground we were playing tag.

"And?" Mr. Fletcher prompted.

"And Russell and Hobart and some others pushed me."

"Is that all?"

I was seven. I couldn't imagine saying the words for what had hap-pened—that one of the boys had rubbed his hand between my legs and said, *I touched her thing*—to this grownup, a man, a man most everyone was scared of.

The window in Mr. Fletcher's office looked out on the playground. His desk was situated so that his back would be toward the window while he worked, but I was facing him and could see outside. Girls stood in groups, talking. Boys ran back and forth.

"Yes," I said.

"Are you sure?"

"Yes."

"Your mother said there was something else."

I could see the spot where the boys had held me down the previous day. If my mother had told him already, why did I have to say it?

I shook my head. I said nothing.

•

In the spring, my parents decided to move. The situation at Elliott was part of the reason, though the neighbors on either side of the house were also contributing factors. The Dyers, on the north, consisted of an extended family: the parents, two sons, a daughter in her thirties, and the daughter's kids. The sons were drinkers, and often my parents would be awakened on Sunday mornings by one of the sons arriving home from a night out and vomiting over the side of the Dyers' porch.

To the south were the Banvilles, the Banville parents and the five Banville kids, who always seemed to have dirt on their faces and food smeared around their mouths. Sometimes Mrs. Banville locked the kids out of the house. You'd hear them banging on the door, begging to be let in so they could go to the bathroom.

•

I understand now—or I can imagine—what motivated the mean boys at Elliott to shove me down on the playground. I can speculate that it involved issues of class and privilege, a sort of resentment that resorted to violence as a way to establish power. Of course they resented me: I was a good student, a smart girl, dressed in stylish little outfits that her mother sewed, who brought to school the kinds of lunches that a concerned mother would create. And they knew I wouldn't fight back; I was passive and quiet. In fact, years later, my mother would tell me about a parent-teacher conference she had with my first-grade teacher, the one who stood in front of the easel during the reading lessons. The teacher remarked on my abilities, my industriousness; but she noted that I also seemed a little detached, that I would sit at my desk staring out the window during lessons. She'd wondered what I was thinking.

Russell and Hobart struggled with reading. They struggled with math. They wore the same clothes almost every day, and Hobart sometimes ate the paste we were supposed to be using for our art projects. I must have seemed like the representation of everything they wanted but didn't—and possibly would never—have.

•

I understand now that the move must have been difficult for my mother. She loved the house on 26th Street, a three-bedroom bungalow with oak floors and built-in bookcases dividing the living and dining rooms. She and my grandfather had spent a whole summer remodeling the kitchen. Still, she could see that the part of Lincoln we lived in was changing: The neighborhood, close to downtown, had been desirable when it had first been established between 1900 and 1920, but now some of the big houses had been divided into apartments. People who let their yards go to rack and ruin were taking over; you lived next to neighbors who vomited off their porches. The time had arrived to move on.

•

The way we found our new house seems like a magical coincidence. All spring and summer, we drove around looking at places that were for sale. The ones we liked were always too expensive. Then, in the early fall, we pulled up in front of a bungalow on the south side of the city. The bungalow seemed like a potential disappointment: not as nice as the bungalow we currently inhabited, and I heard my mother hissing to my father, "Now, they want *how much* for this?"

We got out of the car and stared at the house. My mother sighed. Then, we turned and looked across the street, where a tidy brick Tudor sat in the center of a well-manicured yard. Its clean windows reflected the setting sun. Five enormous oak trees lined the perimeter of the property. It was a lovely house—lovely—and I don't know if I was the one to say it, or my mother, but one of us remarked, "It's too bad *that* house isn't for sale."

A week later, the wish was granted: the Tudor went on the market. My parents could barely afford the asking price, but my grandfather loaned them the down payment, and they sold the house on 26th Street for a small profit they used to pay him back.

In November 1968, on the last trip from what was now the old house to our new house, my mother and I brought the cat, Emerson. I sat in the front seat of our old Cadillac, holding Emerson on my lap.

Of course I'd seen the house we were moving into, but we'd taken side streets rather than the route my mother drove this particular afternoon, down 27th Street and turning east onto Sheridan Boulevard. I'd never been on Sheridan Boulevard, a brick street with an island dividing the east- and west-bound lanes of traffic. I'd never seen such enormous houses rising out of lawns that, even this late in the season, still retained some of the green of summer.

The car's tires rumbled pleasantly against the bricks. The sky overhead was a milky gray. Emerson sat calmly on my lap, looking out the window. We passed house after enormous house. This area, I would come to understand, was the rich end of Sheridan, where the doctors and lawyers and business owners lived. Our house was off the middle-class end of Sheridan, a block north of where Sheridan merged into the more prosaic Calvert Street. So, the place we were moving to was not exclusive but located close to exclusive, and a world away from a neighborhood where children with dirty faces were locked outside.

At the corner of Bradfield and Sheridan was a two-and-a-half-story stucco house with a tile roof. A black wrought-iron fence surrounded the yard. Pots trailing ivy rested on concrete railings that flanked the front steps. Instead of a garage, there was what my mother told me was a carriage house, a two-story building with space for the cars on the ground level and an upper-level apartment where *the help* could live. The trim was painted the shade of turquoise that was my absolute favorite color that year, and when we passed the house—which was, I thought, the most beautiful place I'd ever seen, so remarkable that even Emerson glanced at it—I decided that my goal in life was to live in that very place.

•

I'm convinced that if we hadn't moved, I would be a different person. If we'd stayed on 26th Street, I would have grown up conscious of danger, how it hovered around you, everywhere, how it was arbitrary, capricious. Instead, I learned how the lilacs bloomed every spring on the Sheridan Boulevard island; how it was important, if you had a bag of merchandise from Miller's and a bag of merchandise from Hovland's, to carry the Hovland's bag on the outside so it was the one people saw. My family was living in the new house when my father told me that the Nebraska state capitol was one of the Seven Wonders of the World, and—despite daunting evidence to the contrary—I would believe that for almost thirty years. I also believed the kind of menace I'd known at Elliott wouldn't set foot in the south side of town.

Chapter 3 :: **Lincoln, 1992**

When I first heard the phrase *victim mentality*, I thought it described a person who went through life always looking over her shoulder, terrified that something bad was going to happen. A person who believed the world was filled with constant threat, likely directed at herself, and possibly delusional in the way she always saw herself as a victim.

But the term can be defined in other ways. My friend Tekla told me that she'd learned about victim mentality when a cop spoke to participants in a self-protection course she took. The cop said that victim mentality exists when a person ignores the fact that potential trouble may be present at any time. A person with victim mentality is not careful, not conscious of her surroundings, not aware. She is, in short, a person committed to the illusion of safety.

I'd been that person in Omaha the night I was attacked, oblivious to the risks of taking the alley shortcut, oblivious that a man followed me as I walked along, eating my apple, narrating the story of my walk inside my head. After the attack, I became more careful and conscious of my surroundings. But, years later, back in Lincoln—dear, safe Lincoln—I felt myself slipping. I didn't take stupid chances. I didn't go through alleys in the dark. But sometimes I walked down alleys in the daytime, and occasionally I walked by myself at night. It was difficult to be on guard all the time. It seemed like overreacting to something that had happened years ago, in a different place. It seemed silly.

And then, on September 22, 1992, a girl disappeared.

•

In the fall of 1992, I was thirty-one, a PhD student in the English Department at UN-L, the University of Nebraska in Lincoln. The previous spring, I'd graduated from Nebraska's College of Law. I'd entered law school with the intention of becoming a criminal prosecutor, but I realized by the time I graduated that I was ill suited to the practice of law. For one thing, I wasn't argumentative enough. I had trouble bluffing. I could create a fictional story with no difficulty whatsoever, but I found it almost impossible to make assertions during our moot court arguments when I wasn't absolutely, positively, sure of the correct, true answer. Besides, the only part of the legal cases I found interesting were what we called the facts, the details of what had precipitated the lawsuit: the unsupervised child slamming his tricycle into a woman's leg, the untended tree that split and smashed a car, the question of ownership of a piece of jewelry discovered in an abandoned house. I also found the dress code for women attorneys—suits and hose—completely untenable. Ineptitude and disinterest were difficult to explain, so when people asked why I'd decided against practicing law, I'd tell them, "If I had to wear pantyhose every day, I'd kill myself."

But the deeper truth was that I'd rather spend my time with stories than cases. I was more drawn to narratives than arguments.

The law classes I found most interesting were those having to do with property and real estate, and it occurred to me, in the summer before my senior year of law school, that I should buy a house. This was in 1991, and my yearly income (I was a student, after all, making ends meet with part-time jobs) was about $10,000. Since the conventional formulation is that you can afford a mortgage that's 2.5 times your income, I spent the summer driving around with my realtor and looking at houses in the $25,000 to $30,000 range.

Most of the houses, as you might expect, weren't in the best condition. Most of them were on the north side of town. I did find an old, two-story foursquare with lovely oak woodwork, but it needed a new roof and a new roof was beyond my budget. Finally the realtor and I stumbled across a little bungalow that was, oddly enough, only about three blocks from my childhood home on 26th Street. The house was on a one-block street of nearly identical small houses that had been built in the 1920s for young marrieds just starting out. The lot was minuscule, but the house was sound: new roof, new furnace, and the floors and trim were oak. My father called the police department to check on the neighborhood's safety and was told that relatively little crime happened in the area. If somebody wanted to break in and steal something, the cop said, they'd go farther south or east, where the houses were bigger, nicer, and contained better stuff. The little lower-middle-class neighborhood wasn't worth messing with. My father told the cop his daughter would be living in the house by herself. "The best thing to do," the cop said, "is get a dog."

So I bought the house. My mortgage payments were $265 a month.

The weekend before I moved into the house, I looked through the pets column in the *Lincoln Journal*. Under the "free to good home" listings was a two-year-old male Chow.

A Chow! I thought that was exactly what I wanted.

I called the owner, went to his apartment, and met Yogi. He was a beautiful dog—almost eighty pounds, with thick reddish fur, golden eyes, and a calm, aloof demeanor. "You seem like a nice person," Yogi's owner said. "You can have him."

Walking to my car, holding the leash of my new, beautiful, free dog, I savored this recent run of good fortune, first the house and then the perfect dog. Exactly what I'd wanted dropping into my lap as if all I'd had to do was wish.

•

Occasionally, when I first moved into the house, I'd get the creeps. I'd hear a noise (or think I'd heard a noise) and become convinced someone had broken in through one of the basement windows. Someone was downstairs, crouched in the closet where I kept the storm windows, or waiting behind the door of the basement bedroom. I told myself I was being ridiculous, I was imagining things, but I couldn't sleep until I'd checked to make sure that no one, in fact, was there. So I'd put on Yogi's leash, lead him down the stairs, and we walked around the perimeter of the basement, looking into corners, behind doors, making as many circuits as I needed to confirm that Yogi and I were alone in the house; I was safe.

By September 1992, I'd lived on California Court long enough that I'd become accustomed to sounds the house made when the heater switched on or wind rattled the dining-room windows. I almost never got the creeps any more. Yogi and I had established a comfortable routine; I went to campus in the mornings, then Yogi and I took our daily constitutional down 27th Street and around the Lincoln Children's Zoo, following the bike path that bordered Antelope Creek. Bugs sang in the tall grass that grew on the creek's banks. The llamas at the zoo approached the fence and batted their long-lashed eyes at Yogi. A lonely camel in an enclosure some yards away from the rest of the animals looked cheered when he saw us. People we passed on the bike path often stopped and stared at Yogi. "What *is* that?" they'd ask. We were, after all, behind the zoo, and Yogi did look like a lion. In the evenings, I finished my homework while Yogi lay on the porch, keeping watch over our small patch of lawn. He had a strong sense of discernment and legality—he knew which folks lived on the block and ignored them, but if someone unfamiliar drove up and, even worse, parked in front of the house, where parking was illegal, he'd stand up and bark at them until they moved the car.

Before bed, I brought Yogi inside and locked and dead-bolted the doors. I narrated my behavior to myself: *She turns the deadbolt on the front door. Then, the deadbolt on the kitchen door and the deadbolt on the back door. Perhaps this is an extravagance of caution. After all, Lincoln is a safe place.*

•

September 22 was a Tuesday, and I had a night class from 7:00 until 9:40. The sky was always fully dark when I'd walk back to my car after class was over. Yet on this particular evening, the thought of walking alone in the dark made me uneasy. Why? I wondered, then and still. After all, I'd just be crossing the university campus, then R Street, then the parking lot where I left my car, an area of asphalt that had once held a row of buildings, including McGuffy's Tavern, Dirt Cheap (a record store and head shop), and Chet's Typewriter Sales and Repair, where my parents had bought me my first electric typewriter.

I decided to take Yogi to class with me. He sat upright in the passenger seat of the Corolla on the ride downtown and stared out the front windshield like a person would. I figured the professor and the other students in composition theory would regard Yogi's presence as a manifestation of the English-grad-student eccentricity that everyone else seemed to be cultivating. None of my classmates were from Lincoln; they'd come from Missouri and Indiana, as far away as Massachusetts. As a Lincoln native, I was an outsider among the others, who regarded the town with puzzlement and sometimes a bit of contempt: "What on earth is a *runza*?" they'd ask me. Or "Do you have to memorize the scores of every single football game if you live here?"

One of them, the young man from Indiana, who was a poet, had told me that Allen Ginsberg called Lincoln's O Street "Zero Street" in a poem, a reference I considered a charming error: Ginsberg must have confused the numbered streets, which ran north and south through town, with the lettered streets, which ran east to west. "That's a funny mistake," I'd said.

"I don't think it was a mistake," he said. "Zero means nothing, so what Ginsberg was getting at—"

I was sensitive to criticisms, implied or explicit, of Lincoln, and I could tell that insult was coming, in the form of literary analysis: "Zero means nothing, so what Ginsberg was getting at is that Lincoln is a place of nothingness, or a place where nothing happens."

"Of course it was a mistake," I interrupted and changed the subject.

When Yogi and I walked into composition theory, the other students cooed over the big fluffy dog, and then turned to discussing Foucault. Yogi went to sleep on the floor next to my desk. Pretending to be taking copious notes, I worked on a story based on an interesting rumor I'd heard, that when Hitler planned his takeover of the United States during World War II, he'd chosen Lincoln to be his center of operations.

When class ended, we all packed up our book bags. My female classmates began their usual post-night-class plans of walking together to their cars. I snapped on Yogi's leash and we left Andrews Hall. The campus was quiet: people were either inside the library studying, or downtown at the bars. Yogi and I followed the path that led from Andrews Hall to Love Library. Trees had begun shedding and you could hear fallen leaves ticking along the sidewalk. Yogi's nails snicked against the asphalt. With Yogi next to me, I didn't have to listen for approaching footsteps, didn't have to evaluate the weight of the person walking or judge the relative speed of his approach. If someone menacing came along—and what menacing person would come along?—I knew Yogi would turn his head in that direction and growl low in his throat, his sharp eyeteeth showing when he raised his lip.

We walked past the business administration building. We rounded the corner of the Sheldon Gallery, and I didn't startle like I sometimes did when I saw the statue that looked like a dressmaker's dummy. At night its shadow often made me think, just for a second, that someone was standing there.

We got home around 10:30. We went inside and I locked the doors, as any prudent person would do, then drank a Bud Light and went to bed.

•

On September 22, Scott Barney and Rodger Bjorklund were out looking for trouble. They talked about robbing a bank, but they had an intimation they'd be caught that particular evening. They decided, instead, to execute a fantasy that the two of them had discussed: to abduct and rape a woman. Their grisly motivation was similar to that of Nathan Leopold and Richard Loeb, two friends who, in 1924, kidnapped and murdered a neighbor. (The killing inspired Alfred Hitchcock's movie *Rope*.) "I am sure, as sure as I can be of anything, that is, as sure as you can read any other man's state of mind," Leopold said in a conversation with doctors and state's attorneys, "the thing that prompted Dick to want to do this thing and prompted me to want to do this thing was a sort of pure love of excitement, or the imaginary love of thrills, doing something different."

Barney and Bjorklund drove around Lincoln for hours on that clear

September evening, searching for a suitable victim. The woman had to be alone, away from any potential witness. They needed to be able to snatch her off the street unobserved, as if she'd vanished into thin air.

How many women that night walked past the car with the two men? How many of those women were alone, distracted by thoughts of laundry and homework, boyfriend troubles, unpaid bills—and how many were saved by sheer chance such as a cop car turning onto the street, a couple stepping out onto the balcony of a frat house, a drunk guy stumbling out of an alley?

•

Candice Harms was a freshman at UN-L. On Tuesday, September 22, she'd been studying at her boyfriend's apartment, which was located on 22nd Street, between Q and R, about half a mile from the university. She left the apartment at 11:40 to go home.

She was five foot four, with shoulder-length brown hair. She weighed 115 pounds. She had two part-time jobs, one at Bryan Memorial Hospital and the other at the seed lab on East Campus.

Candice Harms almost always met her curfew. Her mother described her as "an overall good kid." She and her parents were living at Chateau Le Fleur, an apartment complex at 61st and Vine Streets, while they waited for a new house to be built. On September 22, she'd gone to dinner with her parents, who'd just returned from a trip to the Black Hills. Then she went to Todd Sears's apartment. They spent the evening studying, watching television, and talking about a wedding they planned to attend the upcoming weekend. She told him she'd bought a new outfit for the occasion.

Candice packed up her books in time to get home for her midnight curfew. She and Todd stood in his doorway for a goodbye kiss. She started toward her car, then returned to give him another kiss. But she had to leave, of course; she was a good girl, she would meet her curfew, she would never make her parents worry. On the way to her car, she turned and told him to have sweet dreams. He stood in the open doorway and watched while she climbed inside, set her books and purse on the passenger seat, started the engine. She waved. He waved back, standing there in the dark, watching her taillights as she drove north on 22nd Street, headed toward Vine. Maybe he noticed the air that evening was particularly temperate, no chill yet of fall, the way I'd noticed the weather that night in February

1985, the pleasant strangeness of warmth in winter. He'd have known that you had to savor unexpected good weather in Nebraska. You had to give yourself an extra moment to stand outside and appreciate it, because you never knew when it would turn.

Chapter 4 :: **Omaha, 1985**

On the night of February 20, 1985, after the man who'd attacked me had gone off behind the garage, I ran across the street to Jim's condo. I pounded on the door so hard that the neighbor in the next unit came outside to see what was wrong. Her crazy Dalmatian, Sophie, barked and clawed the window. In the dark, the neighbor came toward me, her hands outstretched, and I screamed.

Jim opened the door. I was naked from the waist down, muddy, crying. "Baby," he said. He pulled me into the condo. He shut and locked the door. Then he asked what had happened, though surely he must have known.

"I was raped," I said.

His eyes darkened and his lips blanched, but he stayed calm; he had a naturally unruffled disposition, and he was in his second year of medical school, so he'd cut open cadavers and intubated cats and practiced physical exams on his classmates. Maybe they'd even talked about this subject in class, how to respond to someone who'd been sexually assaulted. He asked what I wanted to do.

I wanted to call my parents in Lincoln and then I wanted to call the police.

"All right," he said. "Call your parents and then we'll go to the hospital. They'll call the police."

First I wanted to take a shower. He told me I couldn't, not yet.

As I remember, the conversation with my parents was brief. My father answered the phone, and I asked to speak to my mother, as she was the one I generally confided in. I told her I'd been raped. After a shocked silence, she asked what had happened, and I said a man with a knife had grabbed me while I was walking to Jim's. We were on our way to the hospital.

Did I want them to drive up?

No, I said. I'd call the next day.

•

That night, before I'd left my apartment to walk to his condo, Jim and I had talked on the phone. I worked the second shift as a reservationist at Ramada Hotel's national call center, and I'd gotten off work early that evening. I called Jim to let him know I'd be over soon and he offered to come get me.

He would've come right away, but I wanted to talk to Abby for a while.

"That's okay," I told him. "I'll walk over in just a bit."

Since we'd become friends in high school, Abby and I loved sharing the most minute details of our lives. Nothing was too small or insignificant to be mulled over and prodded at for a deeper meaning: Had the boy who'd borrowed a pen from Abby brushed her hand on purpose when he took it? Did he fail to look her in the eye because he was shy? Or disinterested? Was *she* interested in *him*? So that evening we sat in the living room with REM playing on the stereo and talked for a good forty-five minutes.

And then I left the apartment.

After Jim and I talked on the phone, he sat at his kitchen table, where he liked to study, looking at the clock and wondering where I was, a little annoyed that I was taking so long. The condo's outer walls were thick; Jim hadn't heard the cut-off scream I'd made when the man first jerked his arm around my neck. Jim never said, "You should've let me come get you." But I knew that mistake was the first in a long line of mistakes I'd made that night.

•

At the hospital, the police told me that in the past year, a number of rapes had occurred in the neighborhood, about one a month, perpetrated by a man who threatened his victims with a knife and who matched the description of the one who had attacked me. They wanted to have an artist put together a composite sketch.

After leaving the hospital, we went back to Jim's condo. I stood in the shower, water pelting on mud that had dried in my hair. The smell of wet dirt reminded me of hair treatments Abby and I used when we were in high school. We bought cans of henna at the Gold's store downtown, and then in the bathroom at my parents' house, we mixed the dried henna with water, scooped the mixture onto our hair, and sat around with the sticky mess on our heads, waiting the requisite time for the color to take. When the henna had dried, you had to soak your hair with water and rub hard to dislodge it.

I'd dried my hair and dressed by the time the police artist arrived, around three in the morning. We sat on the couch, and she showed me little pieces of faces that could be assembled to create an accurate picture. "Was his nose like this? Or more like this?" she asked, offering options.

The composite was fairly easy to put together. After all, I'd gotten a good look at the man's features when he'd first called out and then later on the lot next to the condo. While the composite wasn't an exact representation, like a photograph would have been, it was as close as I could make it.

The artist left at five in the morning. Jim and I went to bed. We lay in the dark with our arms around each other. I touched his face and felt wetness against my fingers. He fell asleep and I stared at the ceiling while the room grew incrementally lighter. I wondered what was going to happen next.

•

The police printed the composite sketch on flyers they posted around the neighborhood and handed out to parking lot attendants and security guards at Clarkson Hospital and the med school. *Wanted*, the flyers said. Abby saw one in the pharmacy school building. She said she hated walking past it on her way to class. "I hate looking at his face," she said. "The bastard."

I took a couple of days off work. I sat in the living room of our apartment, smoking and staring out the window. Across the street was Kaufman's Bakery. I'd loved living across the street from a bakery. Sometimes I'd put a pot of soup on the stove and, while it was heating, run over to Kaufman's to buy cookies for dessert. Next to Kaufman's stood a hardware store, then Sullivan's Bar, and on the corner was Beaton Drug. Years ago, when my mother had lived in Omaha, she'd gone to Beaton Drug's lunch counter for breakfasts of Jewish rye and apple butter. By 1985, the lunch counter was gone, but I went to Beaton's Drug to buy cigarettes.

If you turned right at the drugstore and walked half a block down 40th Street, you'd arrive at Schaeffer Grocery, where my parents had bought me a whole cart full of food when I first moved to Omaha. Schaeffer's was small, and since they didn't let you write checks for cash, Abby and I usually went six blocks farther west to Hinky Dinky.

Jasper's Bar was on our side of the street, so you couldn't see it from inside the apartment. You had to stand on the front deck and lean over the railing to get a good look. I expected the police had questioned the bartenders to see if anyone remembered the man in the canvas coat. Maybe someone even knew his name.

I wondered if he'd been in Jasper's that night in January when Abby and I were there with Jim and his med school friends.

I didn't like the fact that the man knew where I lived. He might have learned I'd contacted the police; he might have seen them inside Jasper's and figured out it was because of me. He might be, at this moment, standing in the hardware store across the street, staring out its window at the apartment. He could be standing there, pretending to look for a screwdriver, waiting for me to step outside. He might be watching the smoke from my cigarette curl toward the ceiling.

I moved to a chair in the corner of the living room where I was hidden in shadow.

•

Two days after the assault, Abby and I sat on the couch after she'd come home from class. We both had cigarettes, even though Abby wasn't really a smoker. I told the story of the rape, again. This telling involved going over every mistake I'd made—not having Jim come get me, failing to look toward Jasper's when I'd left the house, being so lost in thought I didn't hear the guy following me, stupidly not running after he'd called out because I didn't want to look rude.

Abby said, "It's not your fault." She put the cigarette in the corner of her mouth and, squinting, took a little puff. "I went outside last night," she said. "Late. I stood on the deck. I wanted to see if the guy would come after me."

I pictured Abby in her white sweater and jeans, hands resting on the deck's railing, staring out into darkness and shivering in the chilly air. Wind would have lifted her hair as she stood, waiting.

She tapped the cigarette against the side of the ashtray. "I thought what a terrible thing happened to you. It should happen to me, too. I wish it had been me, instead."

We looked at each other with wet eyes, and then I got up and put *Reckoning* on the stereo. That was the album we'd been listening to the night I'd been attacked. We had a game we played with REM: we'd try to discern their unintelligible lyrics and say out loud our interpretations of the words. For instance, Abby heard the first line of "Harborcoat" as "The crowd wrote its letters with their noses worn off."

This afternoon we sat silent, listening and smoking.

Jim finished his classes at five o'clock. Our apartment was located between the med school and his condo, so he stopped and picked me up. We went to his place, made dinner, and watched television for a while. Then he studied and I tried to read a book. I wondered how long I'd be living like this: distracted, jumpy, afraid to go outside by myself, even in broad daylight, smoking too much.

•

On Monday, February 25, five days after the assault, a Clarkson Hospital security guard saw a man walking down the street who resembled the man in the flyer. The security guard flagged down a police cruiser, and the suspect was located and arrested on 40th and Burt Streets around 11:15 a.m. He was taken to the station downtown, and the police arranged a lineup.

An officer called and asked if I could come identify the assailant. "Sure," I said. I put on a skirt and blouse—a casual knee-length skirt and a long-sleeved blouse—and drove downtown.

A counselor from a rape crisis organization was there. She might have been the same one who had showed up at the hospital, wanting to make eye contact and tell me the rape wasn't my fault and that she could help me get through this. I wasn't particularly interested in what the rape crisis people were selling: I resented someone who didn't know me at all acting as if she did, and I found myself recoiling from the camaraderie of victim-hood, the way the terrible event became like a commodity for exchange.

What I wanted was justice—getting the rapist caught and locked up—and the people who could help with this were the cops, with their hand-cuffs and guns. After a moment of uncomfortable conversation with the counselor about how I was doing (*Fine*, I said, and she gave me a look that said she knew I was repressing my true emotions, but that was okay, that was a stage everyone went through), I told the cops I was ready for the lineup.

A couple of the officers were ones I'd talked to the night of the assault, and they explained how the lineup would work. We'd stand behind the one-way glass window, and on the other side, five men would be brought in. Because I'd described the assailant as wearing a cap and glasses, a pair of glasses and a cap would be passed from man to man to try on. I should take my time and study each one. There was no rush; I could take as long as I needed. I shouldn't worry that any of them were able to see through the glass. I was safe here, surrounded by policemen and their guns.

One of the cops said I'd done such a good job with the composite, that's why the security guard had spotted the guy.

Was I ready?

"Yes," I said. I wiped my palms against my skirt.

The men entered the room, facing toward the wall so that I saw their profiles. Then they turned and faced the glass. I looked at the man on the far left, then the next one, and then the one in the middle. A rush of heat rippled from the top of my head down through my torso, and sweat erupted on my hands and shoulders. I stepped back. "That's him, in the middle," I said.

A policeman on the opposite side of the glass was holding out a pair of glasses and a cap.

"Are you sure?"

"Yes," I said.

The man on the left put on the cap and glasses. He gazed in our direction for a minute, then the policeman motioned for him to remove the items and pass them to the next man.

"Look at her neck," one of the cops said.

The second man put on the cap and glasses, waited a moment, then handed them off to the man in the middle. The man in the middle tucked the cap over his hair, slid the glasses on his nose, and looked right at me.

My hands shook. It was him, I was positive. "It's him, in the middle," I said again.

The cop standing next to me was looking at my neck. "Somebody get a camera," he said.

"What's wrong?" I asked.

"Nothing." He sounded delighted. "You know how animals show a physical response when they feel threatened? Dogs' hackles go up?"

I nodded.

"Or porcupines raise their quills? Anyway, your neck broke out in a rash when you saw him—that guy—the one you said is the perpetrator. You'll see it when I get a picture."

Another cop brought in a Polaroid camera. I was instructed to tilt my head back and hold the collar of my blouse away from my neck. I shut my eyes against the flash.

In the picture, you could see red splotches all around my throat. When I showed them to Jim that evening, he said they were ruptured blood vessels. The medical term for them was *petechiae*.

"You're doing a really good job," one of the cops said. He smiled at me, sincerely, I thought, though I knew the fondness they exhibited wasn't personal. That is, they didn't know me well enough to like me or not like me. But as a witness—as a person who could help them do their jobs—I demonstrated all the qualities they could have wished for: Eager to prosecute without coming across as vengeful, articulate, dependable, calm. I'd shed useful clues onto the sheet of paper at the hospital. The pelvic exam had gotten them the rapist's blood type. The composite had been instrumental in capturing the suspect. And now I'd broken out in a rash of fear when I saw him. I hadn't exhibited a moment of doubt, and they'd gotten a photograph of my involuntary physical reaction.

"You're not going to let him out now, are you?" I asked. I was already estimating how fast I needed to walk back to my car to avoid the rapist. I looked at the holster of the cop who'd told me I was doing a good job. I wondered if I should get a gun.

"Oh, no," the cop with the camera said. "Absolutely not."

The lineup men were being led away. I watched the one I'd identified— the rapist—and wondered if he'd heard anything on our side of the mirror, if he'd sensed the jubilant activity, if he knew I was standing on the other side of the smoked glass. Was he beginning to understand what a mistake *he* had made that night in picking me?

Chapter 5 :: **Lincoln, 1969**

I remember this scene so clearly it must be true: My father and I sit on the couch in the living room of the new house on the south side of town, reading the Sunday paper. I have the comics section, and I'm struggling with a puzzle that you have to solve to answer the question posed by a one-frame drawing of a couple, who appear to be teenagers. You can only see their heads; the boy looks serious, the girl's eyes are welling with tears. The question is: Is pity akin to love?

Is pity akin to love? I have no idea. The answer seems like information I need to know, but the puzzle is complicated. I'm having trouble figuring it out, and I feel too self-conscious about my curiosity to ask my father for help.

It's November. The late-morning sun shines in through the front windows and makes bright squares on the carpet. I look up occasionally to admire the fireplace, which is faced with dark marble. We didn't have a fireplace in the old house, let alone one this glamorous.

My father must be reading something in his section of the paper that causes him to remark—or perhaps he's followed my glance to the marble, which reminds him of the many beautiful architectural details in the Nebraska state capitol building, where he had an office as an engineer for the Department of Roads. "You know," he says, "the Nebraska state capitol is one of the Seven Wonders of the World."

I nod. I'm eight years old; my entire frame of reference is the city of Lincoln, and any person could see that the state capitol is the most attractive building in town. It is both exotic and absolutely familiar to me. I call it Daddy's working building, and when my mother and I go to pick him up after work, I walk on the lush green lawns and stand staring up at the limestone façade where the names of Nebraska's counties are etched in stone: Custer, Hooper, Cherry . . . .

And so that morning I came to understand what I would believe as fact for many years, that Lincoln contained one of the Seven Wonders of the World. But I never figured out the answer to the Sunday puzzle and I have continued to wonder: Is pity akin to love?

•

On the first day at the new school, I recognized, almost immediately, that things were different. The second-grade teacher, who was a friend of my parents, assigned a girl to be my guide, to sit by me in class and at lunch, and explain how the days would progress.

Most of the kids wore store-bought clothes. They had clean hair, clean fingernails; no one smelled of unwashed laundry or old cooking oil. The class was divided into three groups for reading lessons. Each group was named after a bird—the Robins, the Cardinals, the Eagles—and when it was time, you'd go to the back of the room and sit in a circle of child-sized chairs with the assigned book on your lap. I realized, possibly not the first day but at least by the end of the week, that the group I'd been put in, the

Robins, was the lowest group. I'd gone from being the smartest girl in the room at Elliott to being at the bottom of the heap here at Calvert.

Before lunch, all the girls lined up and Miss Shaw led us to the bathroom, where everyone took her turn using the stalls and washing her hands. At recess, the girls jumped rope or played four-square on the paved area close to the building. The boys engaged in their yelling games out on the gravel. Teachers stood on the edges of the playground, talking to each other, and during lunch recess, the gym teacher strolled across the gravel, swinging his whistle, a flock of worshipful sixth-graders trailing after him.

•

Shortly after we'd moved to the new house, my mother signed me up for a course titled White Gloves and Party Manners, which was designed to teach girls the proper way to behave at social events and how to set a table. Six other girls were enrolled in the class, which was held at Hovland Swanson, and we met once a week for two months. We were given a booklet that contained reading assignments and exercises, as well as a pair of white gloves we would be permitted to wear at the celebratory final meeting. At the classes, we discussed our reading assignments and practiced performing introductions and making the little curtsies we'd use when we met unfamiliar grownups. We learned the proper technique for removing our gloves: you didn't sink your teeth into one of the forefingers and yank. Instead, you gently tugged at the tip of each finger with the fingers of your other hand to loosen the gloves, and then pulled them off.

Part of being a well-mannered girl required you to keep up your personal hygiene. The book recommended brushing your hair 100 strokes every night. "To make brushing more relaxing," the book said, "lie across your bed, face down, then slowly brush down from the top of your head to the ends of your hair. Switch the brush from one hand to the other after 50 strokes—in that way your arms will not get tired. When you're finished, put your hair brush in a drawer to keep it away from dust." We were also given mimeographed instructions for a weekly *beauty bath* that involved not only bathing and washing and styling your hair, but trimming and filing your nails and cleaning your brushes and combs. If the sink or tub clogged with shed hair, the instructions directed you to pour a bottle of Coca-Cola down the drain.

We learned how to set a table with an extravagant number of utensils and plates, how the salad fork went on the far left side of the dinner plate, then the dinner fork, then the dinner plate (with a salad plate on top of it). Serve from the left, clear from the right. We needed to memorize this, the instructor told us. It was *important information* that would be useful to us throughout our lives.

Put your roll on the bread plate; don't set it on the table. Break off small pieces and butter each piece with your butter knife. You weren't supposed to saw your roll in two (the way my father did) and slather butter on both halves.

It went without saying that you should never chew with your mouth open, reach in front of someone for the salt and pepper, put your elbows on the table, or interrupt when an adult was talking.

When you found yourself in an unfamiliar situation—confronted, perhaps, with a mysterious piece of silverware—it was never a bad idea to simply wait and watch how others responded and take your cues from them.

The final class involved a tea party. We all dressed up for the event and sat around a large table, wearing our white gloves and practicing our good manners. The gloves slipped against the handles when you lifted the teacup to your lips; one girl almost spilled. We made pleasant, stilted conversation. The little cakes served with the tea were on the dry side, but only a person with bad manners would have mentioned such a fact.

After the tea party, we rode the elevator down to the main floor to meet our mothers. We waited politely for the adults in front of us to exit the elevator. Sedately, we stepped onto the polished marble of Hovland's first floor. Ladies browsing through scarves looked over at us and smiled at the little gang of mannerly girls wearing party dresses and gloves, their faithfully-brushed hair shining in the overhead lights.

•

A month after we'd moved to the house on Hillside, on a cold afternoon in December, my mother took me back to Elliott to celebrate my birthday with my old friends. Mother brought cupcakes, and everyone in the classroom was invited, which meant I had to share the treats with the boy bullies, because that was the polite thing to do. You couldn't exclude people you didn't like, and the boys knew that. They could do anything they wanted and still get cake.

After the cupcakes, I went outside with my friends. Since I'd moved, the weather had veered between extremes—day-long snows followed by thaws that were followed by freezes—and so the whole back half of Elliot's playground, over by the fence, had become a sheet of ice, thick and smooth as you'd find in a skating rink.

The girls explained the new game they'd invented to play on the ice. One girl was selected to stand with her arms outstretched. On either side of her, three girls lined up, and everyone joined hands. The six pullers took off running and hauled the chosen one skimming over the ice. It was an excellent game, especially for the one being pulled.

That last afternoon I spent with these girls (Maria and Daphne, others whose names I've forgotten), we took turns in the different positions, but most of the time they wanted me to be the chosen one because it was my birthday celebration, and we must've understood that today was probably the last time we'd see each other. "No, no," they said when I offered to be one of the pullers. "Let us pull you."

The sky had darkened by the time my mother and I left for home. We drove down 27th Street and turned left on Sheridan Boulevard. I was aware that the farther south we went, the nicer the houses became and my understanding of divisions and boundaries—which I refined as I grew older—began to develop on that trip home. We admired the Christmas lights that decorated the windows and eaves on Sheridan Boulevard. We passed the beautiful house with the turquoise trim.

The next day I had lunch at school with my new friends in the room that doubled as the gym when the weather was bad. We sat at the long tables that folded back up against the wall like Murphy beds. In an orderly line, we deposited our trash in the garbage can and slid our trays through the window for washing. No one tried to step on your heel or poke you in the back with the tray; no one hissed threats about what was going to happen after school.

Nothing bad happened after school. I'd walk home across the gravel playground and then the upper playground, which led to the spot where Sheridan Boulevard and Calvert Street merged. I'd cross the street, walk one short block of Sheridan, turn on 42nd, and then I was home. By the time Christmas arrived, I'd moved up to the top reading group. I understood what the term *popular* meant, and who among my classmates belonged in that category and who did not. I forgot the feeling of having to be on guard for unexpected menace. I had left that old life behind.

Chapter 6 :: Lincoln, 1992

On the morning of September 23, 1992, Candice Harms's parents discovered their daughter wasn't in her bedroom. They phoned Todd Sears, who told them that she'd left the previous evening before midnight. Pat and Stan Harms then called the police to report the missing girl.

Meanwhile, around 7:30 a.m., a farmer who owned property along Bluff Road, north of town, saw a blue Corsica parked along the edge of one of his fields. Dew coated the car's surface. He thought the car might have belonged to his brother-in-law, who noticed the vehicle himself that afternoon. The brother-in-law looked inside and saw a stack of schoolbooks on the passenger seat. After finding the owner registration in the glove compartment, the farmers called Mr. and Mrs. Harms, who called the police, who went to Bluff Road about 5 p.m.

To get to Bluff Road, you drive north on 27th Street, far beyond the business and residential districts, so far north that the pavement ends and you hit gravel. A creek runs parallel to Bluff Road, and you can hear birds and bugs that are normally muffled by city sounds. In daylight, it's possible to stand in the middle of Bluff Road, look west, and watch a plane float gently downward, preparing to land at the Lincoln Municipal Airport. You could stand in the middle of Bluff Road as long as you wanted; the traffic is so intermittent as to be nonexistent.

The place where the farmers found Candice Harms's car was about eight miles from Todd Sears's apartment. The Lancaster County sheriff, Tom Casady, said that the car was located "quite a ways from the paved road and residences. There's just no reason to be leaving a vehicle there."

Where was the girl?

Law enforcement officers held down barbed-wire fences, stepped over, and began searching the fields. They walked through knee-high stalks of milo that had bleached out to the color of old paper. The bugs singing in the edges of the fields went silent. The men combed the field until dark. The next day, they brought in tracking dogs, helicopters, and volunteer firefighters to help, but the searchers turned up nothing. It seemed as if the girl had taken her purse, stepped out of the car, and vanished.

The sheriff grew more and more concerned. On Friday, three days after Candice Harms had left Todd Sears's apartment, Sheriff Casady appealed to the public for help. Had anyone seen Harms's car between the time she left her boyfriend's and the time the vehicle was found the following morning? Had anyone seen the girl herself?

Posters appeared around town, in the windows of stores and on the torsos of light posts. They showed a smiling, brown-haired girl, wearing a plaid blouse under a light-colored sweater.

Missing, I read, as Yogi and I walked down 27th Street toward the Children's Zoo. I was wearing a denim jacket; the weather had grown incrementally cooler, the sky a deeper blue than the bleached-out color that hung overhead in summer. While we waited for the light at 27th and Capitol Parkway, I watched cars passing, caught brief glimpses of the drivers inside. I wondered: Did that boy know Candice Harms? Did that woman?

What if the person or persons who knew what had happened drove past? Would the secret knowledge they possessed show, somehow, on their faces? Would I notice?

•

So far, nothing about Candice Harms's disappearance made sense. And this troubled everyone in town, including, I'm sure, many like me who held fast to perceptions of Lincoln that the disappearance upended.

I'd spent nearly my whole life in Lincoln. I believed I understood my hometown the way you understood an old friend, her particular quirks and habits. I knew exactly how long it took to make a round trip from my parents' house to the post office downtown at 10 p.m. (twenty-five minutes, with only brief episodes of speeding). I could describe the kind of clientele you'd find in any of the local bars. I knew the city's divisions and boundaries; I was conscious of the subtext of street names and buildings, how these names conveyed much more than location.

O Street—the Zero Street of Ginsberg's poem—serves as a dividing line through town. The south side of Lincoln is the rich side, the north the poor side. Our house on 26th Street was a mere six blocks south of O, too close, I realized, after I'd lived in the new house a couple of months, to O and therefore too close to the north side. The new house was off Sheridan Boulevard, a street whose name everyone knew, and I learned to use it as a marker to describe where I lived. *Do you know where Sheridan Boulevard turns into Calvert Street?*

Oh yes. Sheridan Boulevard. Yes.

Well, our house is a block north of there.

By the time I was in high school, I'd developed such an aversion to being connected to the poor side of town that I felt myself flinching when I said the word *north*.

•

In the fall of 1992, I still believed that the state capitol was one of the Seven Wonders of the World. You could see the capitol building from the intersection of 27th Street and Capitol Parkway, where Yogi and I paused on our walk toward the Children's Zoo. The capitol was the tallest building in town, a landmark that towered over us, visible for miles. My classmates in the graduate program had begun telling me the bawdy nicknames they'd heard for the capitol: the prick of the prairie, the penis of the plains. I'd never heard any of these terms before. Who was telling them such things?

I thought I understood the town completely. But all that fall, the men who had abducted Candice Harms moved among us, unbeknownst.

Scott Barney, as much a Lincoln native as Candice and I, was twenty-four, six years older than Candice, six years younger than I was. He'd attended Northeast High School but left there during his junior year and spent a brief time at the Bryan Learning Center, which, as anyone in Lincoln could tell you, is where troublemakers went. He left Bryan without earning a high school diploma.

Barney'd had problems with the law seven years earlier, back in 1985, when he was arrested for breaking into ComputerLand and stealing equipment. Juvenile court disposed of the case. Between 1985 and the fall of 1992, Barney had been convicted of petty larceny and numerous traffic offenses. He'd also neglected child support payments for his son, who was four years old, and the child's mother—Barney's estranged wife, Stephanie—had been granted a protection order against him.

In 1992, Barney was living with his father in a three-bedroom brick house on North 55th Street. He'd been working for Rex TV but went out for lunch one day in the spring and didn't return. Even unemployed, he seemed to have plenty of money. He refused to discuss with anyone where it had come from.

Roger Bjorklund, thirty, the son of Seventh-Day Adventists, grew up in Shelton, a small town between Grand Island and Kearney. He'd attended Union College in Lincoln—the Seventh-Day Adventist school six blocks from where my parents lived—from 1989 to 1990, majoring in theology. He maintained a 3.4 GPA. During that time, he worked for Kimberly Quality Care as a home health aide. He left Union College in the summer of 1990. In 1991, he quit Kimberly Quality Care. In 1992, he was living in a small, two-bedroom bungalow on the south side of town with his wife and two daughters.

That fall, Bjorklund, too, seemed to have plenty of money. A female acquaintance who "had known Bjorklund for about a year and had rejected his marriage proposal" said that Bjorklund flashed cash around, loaned money to friends, and took her and her daughter out to expensive restaurants, sometimes twice a day.

Bjorklund and Barney executed a number of robberies during August and September, some more profitable than others. From Rex's TV, they obtained $2,116 on September 16. A week after Candice Harms disappeared, they robbed the Goodyear Credit Union of $31,000.

•

In the weeks after her disappearance, billboards with pictures of Candice Harms appeared around town. Stopped at the light on 27th and Holdrege, I studied her photo. The image on the billboards was slightly different than the plaid blouse/light sweater picture that had first appeared in the newspaper. On the billboard, she wore a red turtleneck with a cream-colored sweater over it. She had on lipstick, and her face appeared a bit thinner than in the other picture. I made the assumption that this photo was her high-school graduation picture; she was a little more dressed-up, standard procedure for the occasion, and I'd been thinner myself in high school than during my first year of college, so I superimposed my own experience on hers.

I could do that in Lincoln, and usually be correct.

Candice's light brown hair was the color of Abby's and worn in a similar style. In fact, she looked to me a lot like Abby in the eyes and mouth.

The billboard said *Missing. Call Crime Stoppers with Any Information.*

Eight of these billboards rose above buildings around town. The citizens of Lincoln drove past them as the days shortened and grew cooler, as the authorities continued to search and found nothing, as those of us who'd memorized what Candice Harms had been wearing the night she disappeared—print blouse, BUM sweatshirt, blue jeans, white sneakers—repeated these details to ourselves.

We said things like, *She must be somewhere. There must be some explanation.* It was difficult to reconcile a girl's disappearance with the idea of Lincoln, Nebraska, as a good place to live, a town much remarked upon for its affordability, civility, excellent public schools. In 1991, with a population of 195,838, Lincoln hadn't had a single homicide.

How does a girl vanish in a place like this?

I began to wonder whether people like my parents, who rarely locked the back door of their house, were delusional or oblivious. Because Lincoln was supposed to be a place of reason and order, a place where people acted in moral and responsible ways, you allowed yourself to take risks because you could. Nights in high school when I couldn't sleep, I'd jog down Sheridan Boulevard at three a.m., never imagining that I could be putting myself in danger.

I liked the dark. I liked the quiet. In spring, the smell of lilacs blooming along the median filled the air. Occasionally a car would go by, and I assumed the driver was probably someone I knew—after all, who else would be in the neighborhood? We were on the south side of town. We were too far away from downtown to see the state capitol, but I was conscious, as I ran, of its presence only a few miles away, the giant statue of the sower that topped the dome and watched over the city. When I got home, and let myself in the unlocked back door that I didn't lock myself, I'd be tired, and calm, and ready to sleep.

Chapter 7 :: Omaha, 1984

In September 1984, a few weeks after I'd moved to Omaha, Abby and I took a long walk. The weather that afternoon felt a little too warm for the season, cloudy, the air still and waiting. The kind of weather, I knew, that came before a cold snap, the kind of weather that meant change was on its way.

We started out around four in the afternoon. We followed Farnam Street east and then cut over to Harney. We passed the house where my mother had rented a room when she lived in Omaha in the 1950s, when she'd been the age I was now. She didn't have cooking privileges in the house, so she took her meals at a nearby lunch counter. The cheapest item on the menu was the "garden sandwich," which consisted of grated carrots and celery between two slices of bread, and that's what she ate every night for dinner.

We passed the Blackstone Hotel, in whose kitchen a chef invented the famous Rueben sandwich. The neighborhood was part business, part residential, with large houses set close together and close to the sidewalk.

We followed Harney all the way down to the Safeway store near 29th Street, where we went inside and bought cans of Diet Pepsi. We stood on the overpass and looked down on the freeway. The Pepsi can chilled my fingers. The sun appeared momentarily. Cars flashed by underneath us.

If we'd kept walking, we would have passed the building that my father told me had been the Killian Hotel, a flophouse his grandfather operated back in the early part of the twentieth century. From my father's description, Johnny Killian sounded like a stereotypical Irishman: short—barely five feet tall—and short-tempered, a drinker. Physically strong, despite his stature. One time when a drunk had refused to leave the premises, Johnny Killian had grabbed the man by the seat of his pants and the collar of his shirt and heaved him out the door.

Had my father actually witnessed this? Or was it family lore—I guessed it was probably family lore, possibly embellished, possibly barely true. Still, it was interesting to think there was a connection between my family and one of the decrepit buildings in Omaha.

Abby and I decided we'd gone far enough, so we headed back. On the walk home, we followed Leavenworth Street, a couple blocks south of Harney. We passed vacant buildings, gas stations, little groceries with bars on the windows. Dust and broken glass lined the gutters. Not much traffic on the street; a clanging sound in the distance. Weeds grew up through cracks in the sidewalk. Here and there sat a house surrounded by a chain-link fence. A bus roared by, shooting a black plume of exhaust into the air. I became conscious of Omaha as a big place, an urban place. You didn't have these miles of run-down blocks in Lincoln, even on the north side of town.

On Leavenworth, the vacant, peaceful, melancholy mood of the afternoon had shifted. Some of the buildings I initially thought were abandoned were actually in business: neon beer signs were coming on in the windows, and men lurked outside the open doors, smoking and glancing up and down the street. They were middle-aged, dressed in mechanics' uniforms or shirts with their names stitched on the chest. The bars were near the sidewalk—in fact, they seemed to be right *on* the sidewalk—and so we had to pass close by these men as we walked. They glanced at us. Some of them narrowed their eyes. None of them smiled.

They probably wondered what a couple of girls were doing, wandering around in a neighborhood that was, perhaps, not exactly the best place to be taking a walk. But how were Abby and I supposed to know this? We'd both grown up in Lincoln, a place where we felt universally welcomed. When you walked in Lincoln, you always looked in the faces of the people you passed—it might be someone you knew—and then, if it wasn't, you'd give a little smile, a pleasant acknowledgment of the other person's existence. Sometimes you'd say hello to strangers, especially older people, because that was the polite thing to do.

Abby and I passed the Stan Olson Bar, the Side Door. The wind picked up, cold enough now that I wished I'd brought a jacket. Bits of trash danced in the gutters. The men inhaled on their cigarettes and blew smoke over our heads.

Abby and I had stopped talking. We marched on, grimly, past block after block of these grubby bars, heading toward 40th Street, where we'd be able to turn north to our apartment. There was no point in crossing the street; bars lined the other side as well. This walk on Leavenworth was the first time I'd felt that wariness I'd known as a child, when we lived in the old house in Lincoln and the mean boys roamed the playground at Elliott. I was conscious of being on high alert, like a domestic animal confronted with something unfamiliar: goosebumps rose on the skin of my arms, the nerves underneath tight; my spine felt stiff and my hearing seemed unusually acute, picking up the whisper of the suddenly chilly breeze as it moved down the tunnel of the street. How odd that a mere three blocks had separated an innocuous neighborhood from one that radiated a sense of menace. In Lincoln, I knew all the neighborhoods well enough to understand where things shifted. Omaha was still a mystery.

Finally we arrived at 40th, where the dilapidated buildings gave way to better-kept ones. The rush-hour traffic was picking up. The menacing mood evaporated.

"That was weird," Abby said.

"I know."

Had I been scared? Almost. At least I'd felt deeply uneasy. At the same time I was a little outraged: we shouldn't have felt threatened at five o'clock in the afternoon! It was practically broad daylight. Of course we knew better than to go walking around North Omaha; that was the black neighborhood, still haunted by the crumbling shells of burned-out buildings from the rioting after Martin Luther King Jr.'s assassination. My father had been in Omaha on business the night the riots began in April 1968. He and his colleague were staying at a hotel by the airport, and to get back to Lincoln, they'd have to go through the area where the rioting was taking place.

My father and his co-worker stayed up until four in the morning, and then they got in the car. The rioting had abated in the middle of the night, and the streets had grown quiet. Burning buildings sent flickers of light into the darkness. The two men sped through the area, glass crunching under the car's tires. They made it safely to the interstate and drove back to Lincoln.

So I was well aware on that walk in 1984 that Omaha possessed a history of violence, of danger, that was greater than anything that had happened in Lincoln. I knew there were places in Omaha to be avoided. Even so, when Abby and I had started our walk that afternoon, the street names were so familiar from my mother's stories of her youth that I'd believed the area was safe. The menacing atmosphere on Leavenworth was a surprise I couldn't quite understand.

But my mother had lived in Omaha over thirty years earlier. The city in her stories was a different place than the one where Abby and I lived now. I wouldn't come to understand how different until February 1985.

Chapter 8 :: **Omaha, 1985**

Perhaps if I'd been thinking about that uneasy walk when I left our apartment on the night in February, I might have been more wary. As it was, I
had recovered the mentality I'd developed growing up, a combination of
optimism and obliviousness, a reliance on details of a certain narrative I
liked to believe: I had an enviable life. I was safe.

My own experience in the aftermath of the assault took on the qualities of familiar narratives, the cautionary tale, the good versus evil story. I didn't realize at the time how unusual it was for the assailant to be
captured so quickly—indeed, to be captured at all—and brought to trial.
According to the Rape, Abuse & Incest National Network, out of 1,000

rapes, 310 will be reported to police; 57 of those reports lead to an arrest; 11 cases are referred to prosecutors; 7 of these cases will result in a felony conviction; and 6 of the rapists will be incarcerated.[1]

Already the aftermath of the attack was defying the odds; the case was moving toward prosecution. On March 6, 1985, a little over a week after Joe N. Griffin was arrested on the corner of 40th and Burt Streets in Omaha, the district attorney held a preliminary hearing. The weather that day was sunny with a chilly, piercing wind. I wore a plaid wool skirt and matching jacket, a navy silk blouse, navy hose, and navy pumps. My parents came up from Lincoln and the three of us drove to the Hall of Justice on 17th and Farnam.

Outside the courtroom, I met Ivory Griggs, the assistant district attorney who would be prosecuting the case. He was a short black man with grizzled hair, in his forties, wearing a natty suit and glasses. Personality-wise, he seemed kind of amped up, like a guy who probably drank a lot of coffee.

Ivory led the way to a conference room off the courtroom. A heavy oak table with a couple of ashtrays on it sat in the middle, surrounded by chairs. He offered coffee, which I accepted, and poured a cup for himself. Then he lit up a cigarette—a Moore, a long brown cigarette that looked like a skinny cigar. I'd smoked a couple of packs of Moores in high school because I thought they made me look interesting and edgy.

I lit up my own Virginia Slims Light.

Ivory said he'd read the statement I'd given the police and reviewed the results of the lineup. He was pleased with the amount of detail I'd been able to provide, and, like the cops, delighted with my reaction when I'd identified the rapist. He explained the sort of questions he'd go over during the hearing. "I'm just gonna ask you to tell the story of what happened that night. Where you were walking, when you first saw this guy, how much he moved you around during the assault." He took a drag on his cigarette. "Whether there was penetration."

I sipped my coffee. It tasted scorched.

Ivory sat on the edge of the table. "The lawyer representing Griffin? It's his first case."

1. Available at https://www.rainn.org/statistics/criminal-justice-system, accessed on January 23, 2017.

"Really," I said.

"White kid. He went to law school at Northwestern. It's a good thing that a white lawyer is representing the black suspect, and I'm representing the state. It keeps people from getting hung up on racial issues. So—" Ivory inhaled on his Moore and exhaled a stream of smoke. "You got any questions for me?"

"Is he going to be here?"

"Griffin? Yeah."

"Is he going to get out?"

"After the hearing?"

I nodded.

"Doubt it," Ivory said. "I've got you and two other women he assaulted to testify." Ivory repeated what I'd heard from the cops, that Griffin was a suspect in at least eight rapes in addition to mine that had happened in the area. "Eight reported rapes," Ivory said. "There might've been others where the cops didn't get called."

Ivory had a detail that the police hadn't mentioned: One of the girls had been stabbed and left for dead. She'd been found in the basement of an apartment building, next to the furnace.

"Is she okay?" I asked.

"She's alive," Ivory said. He tapped out his cigarette in the ashtray.

"Is she one who's going to testify?"

"No," Ivory said.

I asked why more of the girls weren't coming today.

Ivory shrugged. One had moved away, one said she didn't want to go through the difficulties of a trial, another had to work, she couldn't be taking time off. Some wanted to put the whole incident behind them and forget it.

I thought about the girl who'd been stabbed. I didn't know anything about her, not even her name, but I pictured a girl with long dark hair lying on the cement floor. For some reason the room I imagined was the basement of my grandparents' farmhouse out in Eagle, much too innocuous a place for such a scene. I saw the girl lying unconscious on her side next to a furnace, one arm flung out, the other under her body, blood seeping from her wounds, puddling on the floor. Had he thought she was dead when he left her, or did he figure she'd bleed to death before she was found?

He hadn't stabbed me.

I remembered the end of the assault, when he stood to zip his pants and said, "Your jeans are over there." I'd had an intuition that I shouldn't move. That is, it was fine to sit up and reach for my clothes—in fact, sitting up and reaching for my clothes was a good thing to do, to acknowledge that I'd heard him and was responding in a reasonable way—but standing might disturb the equilibrium of the moment, disturb the molecules of air, call attention to me as a person capable of unpredictable activity. And calling too much attention to myself might make him reconsider the decision he'd made, which was to zip his pants, exchange a couple of words, and take off. The man had established in his mind how things would go, and some unexpected behavior on my part might have made him reconsider.

The rape crisis woman probably would've told me I was simply in shock, that's why I didn't move. But I had sensed that I had to stay calm, to stay seated in the mud, holding my jeans, and let him leave before I moved.

I wondered if the girl in the basement had startled the rapist in some way, or if she'd said, "I'm going to the police," because that was something you wanted to say—you wanted vengeance against the person who had just violated you, you wanted him to be afraid the way he'd made you afraid. Or maybe the guy had just stabbed her to see what it was like. What if she'd tried hard to stay calm there in that cold basement as he ground her bare back against the concrete floor, what if she tried to do exactly what he said because he'd promised not to hurt her if she did, and then he'd stabbed her anyway?

"Are you okay?" Ivory asked.

I nodded. I took a drag on my cigarette.

"I want to get this guy," Ivory said.

I nodded again. I wanted to get this guy, too.

•

I wanted to get this guy, but I also wanted answers to some questions. What exactly had been going on in Griffin's head as he stood outside Jasper's two week earlier? Had he gone to the bar in the first place to look for a victim, or had the idea formed in his mind only when he'd seen me leaving the apartment? I began imagining a narrative from his viewpoint:

Griffin is standing on the corner of 40th and Farnam, smoking a cig-
arette, wondering if the damp air is going to turn to mist, when sud-
denly a girl appears, crossing the street, never looking in his direction.
Well, how about that, he thinks. He doesn't make a conscious decision
but simply starts walking behind her, thinking, I'll see what happens
next. I'll follow her for a block and then decide what to do.

The girl walks along, eating an apple, her gray purse banging
against her hip. He wonders how much money is inside the purse. The
girl glances briefly down 39th Avenue before she crosses. A cursory
glance, of course, because at this hour, in a residential neighborhood,
there isn't much traffic.

In fact, much to his relief, there isn't any traffic. Ahead of him, the
girl passes Convenient Food Mart. She has brown hair, curled on the
ends. She turns down the alley that runs behind the store. The alley
leads to a parking lot behind the tall brick apartments that face 39th
Avenue.

No one is around. No one is outside the apartments, no one is in
the parking lot except the girl, who continues to walk, eating her apple.
There's no one at Convenient Food Mart except the clerk inside, leafing
through one of the magazines kept behind the counter, glancing up
every now and then. Of course the clerk has seen neither the girl nor
the man crossing the street; they both cut at too sharp an angle to be
visible from the store's front windows.

No one has seen her, and no one has seen him. He feels as if he's
not even making the decision himself, as if the universe is making the
decision for him by offering this opportunity. He adjusts the cap he's
wearing, pulling it firmly over his hair. He watches her take a few more
steps. She's a small girl—he always chooses small ones, they're easier
to overpower—and clearly not very smart, walking alone down an
alley at 10 p.m.

He has a knife in his pocket. He carries one, just in case. He slips it
out, snaps it open, and presses his thumb gently against the blade. He's
standing a few feet away from the back of Convenient Food Mart, next
to a streetlight. The girl has moved into a pool of shadow and when
she steps out of it, into the light cast by a lamp on the side of the condo
building where she appears to be headed, he calls out, "Hey. Can I talk
to you for a minute?"

Beyond that point, I couldn't make myself stay in his head. I knew I wouldn't be able to ask the questions I wanted to; asking questions was Ivory's job. Right now Ivory was looking at me, like he was waiting for me to say something. "I'm fine," I said.

"All right," he said. "All right."

•

The night of the rape, after I'd called my parents, Jim and I drove to the med center hospital on 42nd Street, about two miles from his condo. He parked the car, and we walked into the emergency entrance. No one was sitting in the waiting room. Jim approached the admitting counter and told the nurse, "I have a rape victim here."

The nurse stood quickly and glanced at me. I saw something in her eyes I couldn't quite identify—a flash of concern, perhaps, or surprise that she was trying to conceal. She called for a doctor over the intercom. "Come with me," she said. She kept her voice calm. I followed her around the counter and into an examination room.

Meanwhile, even though I'd told them on the phone that they didn't need to, my parents were making the hour-long trip up from Lincoln. They assumed I'd be in the hospital closest to where I lived, which was Clarkson, six blocks from my apartment. They stopped there, but no one who'd been raped had checked in.

They wondered where I was.

Someone at Clarkson called the police, who'd been contacted by the nurse at the med center, and so my parents found out where I'd gone. They were waiting when I came out of the examination room. Jim had gone back to his condo and returned with the clothes I'd put on, one of my own shirts I'd left there, a pair of his jeans and some of his too-big socks.

My parents both wore the same shocked and uneasy expression Jim had had when I told him what happened. My mother explained how they'd gone to the wrong hospital—why hadn't I gone to Clarkson, since it was closer?—but now they were here.

The police were there, too, and they wanted me to walk them through the crime scene. Then they'd send an artist to make a composite of the attacker.

In the exam room, when the doctor had finished, he rested one hand on my arm. I'd been staring at the ceiling, but I turned to look at him. He was older than I was, probably in his thirties. "I'm sorry this happened to you," he said. "It's not your fault. You know that, don't you?"

I nodded. Tears welled in my eyes. He said, "You can stay here as long as you need to."

I nodded again. He left the room. I stared again at the ceiling, still hearing the words *not your fault*.

Of course it was my fault. I hadn't been paying attention; I'd walked down an alley alone after dark. What did I expect?

I felt the tears sliding down the side of my face and into my ears.

But I could make an effort to believe—or pretend to believe—what the doctor said. Lying here weeping in the hospital room seemed like the sort of clichéd scene you'd see in a movie. I took a deep breath and forced myself to calm down, using a strategy I'd employed for years: whenever I felt on the verge of crying. I thought of a refrigerator, clean, white, and empty. I kept the image of a refrigerator in my mind as I dressed and left the exam room. I pictured the wire shelves, the closed door of the freezer, the little compartment for butter. Now, standing in the waiting area with the police and my parents, I felt I could maintain control by focusing very doggedly and narrowly on several specific things I wanted: showing the police the crime scene, a cigarette, a shower. I was walking an emotional tightrope. Anything, especially any comfort offered by my parents, would topple me.

I assured my parents they didn't have to stay in Omaha, that there wasn't really anything they could do. They argued a little, but eventually gave in and drove back to Lincoln.

The cops met us at Jim's condo. I wanted to take a shower—my skin itched inside my clothes; it felt coated with dirt and dried sweat—but first I had to point out exactly where everything had taken place. Even though we were trying to be quiet, since it was two in the morning by now, we made enough noise that a few people stepped out of their units and onto the second and third floor balconies and looked down. I didn't want to be the object of strangers' speculation. Was everyone going to know what happened to me?

I led the three cops back to 39th Street. Their leather holsters creaked, a sound that made me think of saddles. *Here is where I turned to go behind Convenient Food Mart.*

Here is the light the guy was standing under.

One of the cops snapped pictures. The others swung the beams of big flashlights along the ground and up the walls of the building.

Here's where I was when he called out. Here's where he grabbed me. There's the apple I dropped.

The cop took a picture of it.

Here's where he first pushed me on the ground and asked for money.

In the mud lay the items I'd dumped from my purse: dimes and pennies, my mother's old I Like Ike buttons, a wrapper from a toothpick. Part of a footprint was visible in the mud. The grass was flattened where the attacker had pressed my shoulders against the ground.

We crossed the street to the garage. Again, the mud held various prints, and the cop snapped photos.

Behind the garage, I pointed east to show the direction the man had run, and one of the cops made his way down the incline, the beam of his flashlight swishing back and forth.

Later, after the rapist was apprehended, I learned information about him that would allow me to put together a story of what happened—of what might have happened—after he left me sitting in the mud.

He headed home after the assault. After a few blocks traveling through backyards, setting the occasional dog to barking, he cut over to Dodge and followed Dodge to North 33rd Street. The wind pushed his unbuttoned coat out on either side of him like wings. He noticed that the wind didn't have the sharp teeth of winter. Would it be an early spring?

He paused in Gifford Park and sat on one of the picnic benches, smoking a cigarette. He thought how careful he'd been—keeping his hair covered with the cap he now took off (it really was too warm an evening to be wearing a hat), staying in the backyards for several blocks to dilute the connection between his presence in the neighborhood and the attack. He couldn't remember if he'd threatened the girl to not contact the cops. He was pretty sure he'd said, "You go to the cops, I'll know, I'll come after you and make you wish you hadn't."

He'd done this thing before, and he was always careful. He'd been locked up earlier, from age twenty-two to until April 1984, when he was twenty-seven, for burglary, escape, failure to appear. He'd been out of prison for almost a year now, and he wasn't going back.

He finished his cigarette, threw the smoldering butt into a puddle of melted snow, where it sizzled and went out. He got back on North 33rd and followed it to Lafayette Avenue, to the two-story house where he lived with his mother, stepfather, and stepbrother. It was a little after ten-thirty when he arrived home. His stepfather was sitting in the living room, watching television.

Did the stepfather see anything strange on the face of his stepson? Did he have any idea what he'd done?

•

In the conference room, Ivory said, "I wonder if you could do something for me."

"Sure," I said.

"One of the other girls that's going to testify, Tara, she's pretty scared about this whole thing and she's been having some second thoughts. Maybe you can help her understand why it's a good idea to go ahead with it."

"Sure," I said again.

Ivory left the conference room. Time passed. I smoked another cigarette, even though I was trying to cut back to my usual regimented schedule of smoking, wherein I allowed myself exactly seven cigarettes per day: one with my morning coffee, one while I waited for my nail polish to dry, one before I went to work, one on my afternoon break, dinner break, on the drive home, and a final one with Jim at his condo, which we smoked in the bathroom with the fan on so the whole place wouldn't smell like cigarettes.

Already today I'd had four.

Ivory returned with the two other witnesses. They were small, like I was, between five foot and five-three, probably weighing less than a hundred and fifteen pounds. Diane had short, strawberry-blond hair; Tara's hair was brown and shoulder-length. She wore glasses. They both wore pants, the sort of pants that were a notch less casual than jeans, and sweaters.

Ivory said, "We'll start in a little bit. I'll be right back."

He left, and we all looked at each other. Diane sat down at the table and pushed the ashtray back and forth between her hands.

Tara looked young. Young, and anxious. When she lit a Marlboro Light, I saw her hands shaking. I said, "Are you scared?"

"Yeah."

Diane slid the ashtray toward her.

She was frightened, Tara explained, to have to look at the guy again; she was afraid he'd get out, come after her, and do something terrible. Her hands shook the whole time she talked, and she kept glancing around the conference room.

"Look," I said, "the best way to make sure he doesn't get out is to testify."

Diane nodded in agreement.

Tara drew on her cigarette. "You're probably right," she said, doubtfully.

"No, really," I said. My father had once told me I was bossy, and I was conscious now of trying to be convincing and supportive, rather than strident and pushy. I sat back in my chair and made sure my voice wasn't too loud when I spoke. "It's what we have to do. You don't want him to get out and attack somebody else, do you? When that's something we can prevent by testifying?"

Tara tapped out her cigarette in the ashtray. She stared down at the table for a moment, and then looked up. The lenses in her glasses were thick. She was probably dressed in the nicest clothes she had, trying to make a good impression. "You're right," she said. She still sounded not fully convinced, but not quite as dubious as when we first started talking.

Ivory returned. He was smiling and confident. "Everybody ready?" he asked cheerfully.

Tara nodded. Diane nodded. I said, "Yes. We're ready."

Chapter 9 :: **Lincoln, 1992**

A friend once said that aimless driving or walking is the sign of a troubled mind, and I thought that idea seemed especially true in the fall of 1992, when I spent a lot of my spare time wandering around Lincoln, walking or driving past the landmarks of my childhood and places I remembered from college parties. Candice Harms was still missing. Articles appeared in the paper every couple of days, news that was essentially no news: the police had no leads. The boyfriend was interviewed, and interviewed again. On campus, there was talk of installing emergency phones.

In the chilly sunlight of an October afternoon, I walked south from campus toward downtown, students and businesspeople on the sidewalk around me. Certain stores had been such significant locations in my life, places I went to purchase specific items, of course, but also places where I'd gone to kill time; where friends had worked; where I'd learned things—such as the proper way to set a table—that had stuck with me my entire life. The stores offered a direct connection with a past that seemed, especially in that fall of 1992 when Candice Harms had disappeared, safer and more refined, and the store I missed the most was Miller and Paine.

The Miller and Paine building stood on the corner of Thirteenth and O, right in the heart of downtown Lincoln, eight stories of modestly gothic architecture. Known locally as Miller's, the store had gone out of business in the 1980s, and by 1992, the building had been remodeled into office space. Blinds hung in the windows where mannequins once posed, showing off the latest fashions, the mannequins themselves—I imagined—consigned to the city dump.

Growing up, I'd been in Miller's at least once a week, either shopping or visiting my mother, who'd worked there off and on for most of her adult life. We ate chicken pot pies and cinnamon rolls in Miller's tearoom on the fifth floor. Some of the waitresses who served us had been there twenty or thirty years, and they walked slowly, their wrists bent under the weight of heavy china plates and bowls. My grandmother—my mother's mom—who died long before I was born had worked in the tearoom when she was young, and my mother went on to work there when she was in high school. And when I was in high school, I waitressed at the tearoom in the Miller's store in Gateway Shopping Center, the mall on the east side of town.

Everything connected. In Miller's, you could think of your life as grounded, anchored in familiar and comforting details.

On Miller's second floor, the women's restroom consisted of an enormous powder room and an adjoining room containing at least thirty or forty toilet stalls. Four of the stalls had miniature toilets, designed especially for children. The overhead lights cast a dim golden glow over the marble walls and porcelain sinks. As a child, I was fascinated by a smaller room near the entrance to the powder room, called the Ladies' Lounge. The lounge contained four cots, made up with sheets and thin blankets, tissue paper on the pillows. Women who had tired from shopping could lie down and rest in the dark.

The Bridal Department had been on the second floor. My mother worked as the bridal consultant for a couple of years when I was in junior high, and I used to ride the bus downtown and go to lunch with her, then spend the afternoon sitting on a step in the back stairwell no one ever used, reading a book I'd checked out from the library down the street. One slow afternoon when I was lingering around the bridal department, waiting for Mother to return from a managers' meeting, her assistant—a blond girl in college—suggested that I try on a wedding gown.

"Just for fun," she said.

"Okay," I said.

One of the boys from Shipping and Receiving pushed his canvas cart toward us. A handsome boy: dark hair, green eyes, tall. He asked if there was anything that needed to be delivered to the Gateway store. Cathy shook her head. "Not today." The boy and his cart moved off toward the freight elevator.

Briskly, Cathy went through gowns on the rack that held the smallest sizes and located one she thought would fit. I followed her into the dressing room, which was large as a bedroom and furnished with chairs and benches so that doting mothers and grandmothers and friends could sit and evaluate the various dresses the bride-to-be tried on. Mirrors covered the walls from floor to ceiling. I removed my clothes—the hippie buffalo sandals everyone wore that year, a red denim jumpsuit and plaid blouse—folded them, and set them on one of the benches. I stood in front of the mirror, trying to avoid looking at my reflection: a very slightly chubby girl in cotton underwear, a white lace bra in the smallest size Miller's carried, beige knee socks.

Cathy slipped the yards of satin and net over my head. "Close your eyes," she said. "I'll tell you when to look." She pulled the dress's zipper up, its teeth cool against my back. The dress was heavy—heavier even than a winter coat—and the fabric was smooth and slick against my skin. I felt her arranging the train around my feet. She settled a headpiece on my hair and pulled the sheer fabric of the veil in front of my face.

"All right," she said. "You can open your eyes."

I looked in the mirror. I was too flat-chested to fill out the bodice, but everything else about the dress, I thought, was perfect: the sleeves puffed around my arms, panels of lace ran from the neckline to the waist, and satin pooled extravagantly around my feet.

"Put your hands at your waist," she said, and demonstrated the pose a bride-to-be would adopt for her wedding photograph, with her right hand against her stomach and her left hand on top of it. "You put the left hand on top so the engagement ring shows."

I arranged my hands. In the mirror I looked—almost—like one of the real brides whose photos hung on the walls of the bridal department, girls who'd bought their wedding dresses at Miller's, had their hair styled in the Miller and Paine salon and their pictures taken in Miller's photography studio. And now, here they were, captured in their connection to the very department store in which I stood, fourteen years old, pretending I was a grown-up girl, a bride.

•

If Miller and Paine had still been in business in the fall of 1992, I thought, that's probably where Candice Harms would have bought the dress she planned to wear to the wedding she and Todd Sears talked about attending the last night they saw each other. But all the downtown stores were gone by then. She probably went to Younkers at Gateway.

How could I presume to know where Candice shopped? Somehow it seemed a natural assumption based on my understanding of Lincoln. I'd learned to read details—someone with her arms loaded down with Hovland's bags likely had more disposable income than someone carrying a sack from JC Penney's—and there was comfort in how such details fit together.

For instance, the names of schools in Lincoln would be meaningless to someone living elsewhere, but for us, they conveyed significant information. We could summarize the population of each of the four public high schools in a word or two. Lincoln High, the oldest high school in the city, had originally been the place that children of the old-rich families in town had attended. Now, Lincoln High meant hoodlums and less-affluent students who lived too close to, or in, the north side of town. Northeast High was the second oldest school, on the far north side of Lincoln; Northeast was working class, Northeast was gearheads. My school, Southeast, had been built in 1955, and was now the school of the old-rich and middle-class kids. East, the newest school, was what we called new rich. The girls at East wore plastic jewelry while those of us at Southeast wore gold-plated chains around our necks, and little chip-of-diamond promise rings from our boyfriends on our fingers.

The best lineage, from grade school to junior high to high school, was Sheridan-Irving-Southeast. I was Calvert-Pound-Southeast, which wasn't as good, but was still nothing to be ashamed of. It was nothing like Elliott-Whittier-Lincoln High, which would have been my lineage if we hadn't moved.

To someone not living in Lincoln, these names were simply abstractions. To us, they told someone's life story—where in town she lived, how much money her family probably had, where she shopped, what her chances were for going to college—in three words.

Later I'd wonder whether Scott Barney had learned to read these details as I had. Was the information I took such comfort in understanding the very same knowledge that allowed him to locate a victim to fulfill his and Roger Bjorklund's grisly fantasy?

•

On that October afternoon shortly after Candice Harms's disappearance, I went inside Miller and Paine, now remodeled almost beyond recognition as office space. The elevators and escalators had remained in their original locations, and I stepped on the escalator that connected the first and second floors. This escalator, I remembered, had a little lurch about a third of the way up, as though the belt were going over a speed bump. The lurch was still there. My own unknown grandmother may have been familiar with it, riding up this very escalator decades earlier, wearing her waitress uniform.

On the second floor, the big open space—a sort of lounge I remember filled with chairs—that you crossed on your way to the ladies' room had been blocked off by walls. Little flickers of recollection sparked as I walked around the floor: Hadn't the juniors department been here? Or was that upstairs? Was this where the bins filled with alphabetized rows of record albums used to be?

A woman came out of one of the offices and looked at me evenly. She probably wondered what I was doing, wandering around as if I were looking for merchandise.

Riding the escalator back to the first floor, I recalled a distinct moment from years earlier. The notions had been located on the main level in the area between the escalators, and I could remember looking down at the top of my mother's head as she stood in front of a button display, holding a sample of fabric and reaching out for a card of buttons. I was conscious of the past hovering beneath the present in the familiar smell of the building, the familiar feeling of the handrail beneath my fingers, the inconsequential recollections that occurred to me as the escalator slid quietly along its tracks.

What other minor, half-remembered or entirely forgotten encounters had happened in this place while it was still a department store? I began speculating: I pictured Candice Harms as a little girl shopping with her grandmother for a special Sunday school dress and then stopping for a treat of cinnamon rolls and milk in the Tearoom. The man, whoever he is (he who knows what has happened to Candice Harms now in the fall of 1992), enters the store, looking for things to shoplift. He rides the up side of the escalator and feels the lurch at the point he's come to expect. He looks across to the down side of the escalator (where I stand as I'm thinking this) and sees a brown-haired girl next to an older woman, a momentary encounter he will forget almost as soon as it has happened. The little girl won't notice. The grandmother won't notice.

I step off the escalator. I cross the marble floor to the revolving door that opens into the foyer that leads to 13th Street. It was likely that Candice Harms had, at some point in her life, crossed this foyer herself and stepped out into the air of a fall afternoon in Lincoln. Where was she now? Why could we not find the clues that would bring her back?

•

In college, Abby and I went to parties at the Cherry Hut, a decrepit sort of social hall out by the Lincoln Airport. The Cherry Hut—named, according to one story, because of the flashing lights (cherries) on top of the police cars that were continually called out, in the forties and fifties, to break up fights—was some blocks off Cornhusker Highway, tucked among houses in the Airpark neighborhood. It was a single big, barnlike room with wooden floors. In the dingy bathrooms, shower curtains—rather than doors—hung in front of the toilets. At the parties, there would be a couple of kegs placed randomly, often a band playing on a makeshift stage in one corner. There was no sign for the Cherry Hut, and we could never remember the precise cross streets of its location; whenever Abby and I went there, we'd find ourselves driving around, trying to remember if various landmarks looked familiar, stopping every now and then to get out of the car and listen for the noise of a party.

In the fall of 1992, I drive around Airpark, looking for the Cherry Hut, remembering a summer night years earlier: I'm standing in the parking lot, kissing a boy I'd met the previous week at a party. Lilac bushes surround the parking lot. It's too late in the season for the flowers themselves, but the leaves are dark green, fluttering in the hot breeze. Abby comes outside to check on me, sees us, goes back inside to the party.

I turn on streets with unfamiliar names; Airpark was a neighborhood we never went to except for Cherry Hut parties. But after half an hour of looking, I decide that either the Cherry Hut is gone—torn down—or else I have truly forgotten where it is.

•

I'd met the boy I was kissing in the Cherry Hut parking lot at a party near 40th and South. I drive past the house, which was the family home of a guy a couple years ahead of us in high school. In July 1981, I stood in the backyard with Abby, next to the keg. A tall, dark-haired boy with green eyes crossed the lawn toward us. He asked me, "What's your name?" He wore Converse tennis shoes, Levis, an old bowling shirt he'd probably picked up at the Disabled American Veterans Thrift Store over on 27th and Vine. His face had seemed vaguely familiar to me. I thought, for some reason, that we'd seen each other before, but not talked.

I told him my name. I said, "And who are you?"

"Oh," he said and smiled. He had straight white teeth. "I'm Prince Charming."

A smart-ass, I thought. Just the sort of boy I liked. We stood next to the keg, carrying on a bantering conversation. He was a couple of years older than I was; he lived in the house on J Street where parties were always happening.

Maybe I'd seen him at one of those parties.

Prince and I hook up a couple of times that summer, and then I start dating someone else, and a few months after that, Prince Charming moves away from Lincoln to Phoenix, and I won't see him again for almost thirty years.

•

The house on J Street—where Prince Charming lived, with a couple of other guys—is close to my house on California Court, so it's easy to swing by on my way home from campus. It looks like a normal house, a little run down, smaller than I recalled. I remember parties there, a band set up in the dining room, the living room packed with people, the keg in the kitchen. It had seemed like an almost mythical place back in the 1980s, the site of all those parties we would reminisce about for years. And events we wouldn't—couldn't—talk about again, or even admit to ourselves. Miller's, I realized, seemed permeated with only gentle ghosts of the past. What ghosts would I meet in the house on J Street now?

Chapter 10 :: Lincoln, 1980s

My undergraduate experience in Lincoln was probably similar to the experiences of girls in any number of college towns during the 1980s: you attended classes, some of which were more interesting than others, and you read books, wrote papers, took tests. Nights, you went out with friends, after the complicated ritual of getting ready, which involved curling your hair with hot rollers, cementing it in place with hairspray, putting on Levi's (boys' Levi's, because it was uncool to wear girls' jeans, the way it was uncool to ride a girl's bicycle) and one of your mother's retro cardigans over an oxford shirt. Probably at the very moment on Friday evenings when I was spritzing Halston perfume on my wrists, there were girls in Iowa City and Lawrence and Madison doing the very same thing. That said, we—those of us in Lincoln who met up at parties and in the downtown bars—thought our experiences were unique, as if we were Lincoln's version of the Lost Generation in Paris. We believed the bars we frequented had to be more interesting than bars in other places, our parties wittier and more hilarious. Now hindsight illuminates all too painfully those moments of menace that we overlooked or renamed or repressed at the time.

There was a guy, Jason, who'd been a year ahead of us in high school. He went to the same parties Abby and I and our other girlfriends did; he was one of the group of guys we hung out with at the Drumstick and Sandy's bar. In college, we started hearing stories about him, what he'd been doing to girls.

We heard about what he'd been doing to other girls after it had happened to us.

These incidents are disturbing to remember, and I have trouble finding the best way to tell them. It's more comfortable to hide behind the permissible literary strategy of conflating events and third-person point of view and present the story this way:

It's Saturday night at a party, the sort of party that could have happened at Jason's fraternity, or the house on 40th Street, where I met Prince Charming. This particular party is in the house on J Street, where one of the guys Prince lives with is Jason's elder brother. The Police are blasting from the stereo, there's a line at the keg in the kitchen, cigarette smoke hangs in the air. Two girls stand in a corner of the living room, talking. One is drunk and laughing so hard she's having trouble finishing her sentences. Jason sees this from across the crowded room, takes a drink of his beer, and walks over. He integrates himself into the conversation and the girls will admit—at the moment, even later—that they are flattered to be sought out. After all, he is a charming guy, good-looking, friends with the other charming and good-looking guys. He touches the arm of the laughing girl. He gives her elbow a little squeeze, his fingers a pressure against the bone she can feel. He whispers in her ear, something sweet and innocuous like, "You have a cute smile."

When the friend goes off to get another beer, he says, "I want to talk to you about my girlfriend. She doesn't understand me. I can tell you understand me." Come here, he says, and she follows him toward the steps that lead to the basement. Does the girl have any idea of what he has in mind?

She feels special at having been sought out—chosen—by this cute guy, one of the popular boys in high school, now in the right fraternity in college.

She thinks she understands these guys, all of them, who are people she might refer to as friends. They've all known each other for years, if not intimately at least peripherally. They walked the same halls at Lincoln Southeast, they understand how things in the town fit together, how certain people at the party connect to certain buildings—for instance, one of the boys they pass on the basement stairs is the grandson of the man who founded the big sporting goods store on O Street. If the two of them, the girl and Jason, had a conversation about places in Lincoln, they'd mention the same landmarks, they'd scoff at the same activities, like cruising on O Street, which the kids from the north side of town do on weekends, driving their gearhead cars up and down the strip, pulling into the Arby's parking lot at 56th and O and waiting with their headlights on, engines idling. The kids on the south side of town are too sophisticated to cruise O. Instead, they go to parties.

The girl's friend is upstairs in the kitchen, talking to Prince Charming.

The noise of the party fades as they move into the basement, which is divided into two rooms: in the main room, there are couches and chairs, a couple of people sitting around, smoking and drinking beer. The other room is a sound studio, where the guys who live in the house—who are in a band that sometimes plays at the Drumstick—go to record songs. Jason knows all about the room because his brother lives here. The sound studio has a door. He says to the girl, "Let me show you this place. It's amazing!"

The girl follows Jason into the room. He shuts the door.

There's a couch against one wall, and Jason sits down and pats the cushion next to him. "Come over here," he says. "You're too far away."

So she sits next to him, and then he starts kissing her, which she permits for a minute or two, but then he puts his hands on her breasts. She protests: "You have a girlfriend!"

"That doesn't matter," he says. "She doesn't understand me. I told you."

His fingers work at the buttons of her blouse.

She says, "I need to get another beer." She keeps her voice low; she isn't sure if the people in the main part of the basement are still there, if they can hear her.

"You can get one later. You have such pretty hair." His hands cup her face. He kisses her. Hard.

She pulls away. "I need to go to the bathroom."

Now he reaches for the buttons of her Levi's. He says, "I just want to make you feel good."

Meanwhile, the girl's friend, who is still upstairs in the kitchen, feels a little nudge of uneasiness: the girl has been gone awhile. Worse, she's with Jason, and the friend knows what Jason is like. She had her own experience with him the previous summer, during a party at the house over on 40th Street, in a car parked on the street by the Bryan Learning Center, the school where troublemakers got sent.

In the basement, the girl says, "I've got a curfew. I have to leave."

"No," Jason says. "I'm not letting you leave until you give me what I want." He takes her hand and holds it against the front of his jeans. He says, "If you don't, I'll tell everyone what a slut you are."

The girl is drunk, yes, and surprised at his persistence. Surprised, but not yet frightened. "Come on," she says. "Cut it out."

The friend upstairs knows what Jason is like. Charming, persuasive, persistent, then mean. In the car outside the Bryan Learning Center, he'd pressed her hand against his jeans and said, "I bet you can't even get me hard." A challenge and an insult, the suggestion that she was not sexy, not competent, that she didn't know what she was doing, a low opinion of her he'll hold unless she proves him wrong.

The girl in the basement is aware of the people on the other side of the closed door. The people on the other side of the closed door limit her options. What is she going to do, scream? Storm out of the room with Jason following in a leisurely way, shrugging and smiling at the other partygoers, making a face that says, *What did I do? What's her problem?* That would certainly get people talking, about how she's a prick tease, how she can't hold her liquor, that she's a girl who doesn't really fit in with the rest of them, that you're better off avoiding her at parties. She knows how people get reputations, and she's young enough to believe that being known as a bad drunk and a prick tease might ruin the rest of her life.

Later—even as soon as the next day, relating the story to her friend—she'll realize the fallacy of her thinking, but at this moment, she feels helpless, trapped.

I know, the friend will say. That's exactly how I felt, too.

So the girl gives in, lies motionless beneath him on the couch, staring at the ceiling of the sound studio and waiting for him to finish. She's drunk enough that she can think, *Maybe this really isn't happening. Maybe this doesn't really matter.*

The sex is an exchange made so she'll be able to leave the room with her dignity intact.

•

The girl in the basement with Jason is Abby. The friend upstairs in the kitchen is me. I know what happened to Abby because she told me the following day, during one of those long phone conversations we'd been having since we became best friends in high school. We must have known the term "date rape" because we began referring to Jason, between ourselves, as The Date Rapist. In the same way I referred to cigarettes as cancer sticks, there was something oddly light-hearted in the way we used the nickname, as if it was innocuous as the nicknames of other boys we knew—Paddy, Westy, Uncle Joe.

The Date Rapist story is a difficult one to tell because it's hard to explain certain aspects of our behavior in a way that makes sense.

If I told the story in a chronological fashion, events unconflated, using the first person, it would go like this: At a party at the house on 40th and South, I started talking to Jason. It was the summer after I'd graduated from high school, a few weeks before I went to college. He said he wanted to see my car—I drove a 1965 Cadillac my parents had had for years—and so we left the party, crossed the street, and sat in the front seat of the Cadillac, talking for awhile, and then kissing. He pressed my hand against the front of his jeans. I pulled away. He said, "I bet you can't even get me hard." There was a mean undercurrent to his voice. I should have pushed him away and gotten out of the car. But I was, in some ways, still the girl who'd been touched on the playground at Elliott and couldn't tell the assistant principal what the boys had done. I'd imprinted on the behaviors of submitting and not telling. I didn't get out of the car.

I wrote down in the journal I was keeping that summer what had happened: I noted that the incident wasn't exactly rape because I had, after all, *given in.* I told Abby. Knowing that I'd told Abby, you might imagine that she'd have had reservations about going off with Jason to hear about his girlfriend. You might think (and you are right) that I should've followed along or gone to check on her when she was in the sound studio.

I might explain our response from a psychological angle—that we felt ashamed by what had happened (which is true) and ended up repressing the incidents because they conflicted with the way we wanted to understand the narrative of our lives: the jovial parties, the safety of the known. The idea of the safe, happy life and the actuality of what a boy we knew might do were in such conflict with each other that it was impossible to hold both of them in our minds without going crazy. One of the ideas had to be forgotten, or altered.

Years later, after I'd gone to law school and studied torts and learned about the economics of harm, I saw that we'd also responded to the situation by employing a cost-benefit analysis: the benefit of confronting Jason or making generally known what he'd done would be outweighed, we believed, by the cost of public shunning. And so we put the incidents aside—bad things that had happened, on par with an unfortunate clothing purchase that you never wore, gave to the Goodwill, and put out of your mind.

Jason's coercion happens again—a closed door at a party, this one at the Phi Delt house, another friend of ours feeling trapped, unable to leave—but all of us keep our dignity intact. We continue to go to parties, where we run into Jason, exchange a few words, move on. We go to the bars we've always gone to since we turned twenty-one, the legal drinking age, with the express purpose of running into the guys we've known since high school. We refer to them as our drinking buddies. We meet up on Friday afternoon at Sandy's, which sits on the northwest corner of 14th and O Street in Lincoln. Decades earlier, the place was called the Acme Chili Parlor, and my father and his own friends hung out there when they were in college.

No outsider would likely have found Sandy's inviting with its grubby exterior and wooden booths whose varnish turned tacky in the summer heat. Patrons were permitted to write on the bar's walls with chalk, and the rough wood was covered with the Greek letters of fraternities and sororities, names of couples, obscure insults and phrases. Sawdust from the shuffleboard table next to the booths coated the floor.

Sandy's patrons were a mix of college students and locals. The college students were primarily from Lincoln and Omaha, primarily Greek affiliated. The locals were old guys with alcoholic tendencies, distended stomachs, broken veins on their noses and cheeks. The locals sat at the bar; the students sat in the booths.

Friday afternoons, Sandy's ran happy hour specials from 3:00 to 6:00. Elk Creeks—Sandy's signature cocktail, a delicious mixture of rum, gin, and vodka, mixed with orange juice and a shot of soda water for fizziness—were a dollar a glass. One winter afternoon, the snow falling in sheets, stands out as clearly to me now as the day it happened.

We begin lining up outside at 2:30, stamping our feet on the sidewalk to keep warm, snowflakes melting on our lashes. Finally the bartender opens the door and we file in. Abby goes to the bar to order drinks and I dodge around the other patrons to snag the booth we like, in the back, by the big window that looks out on O Street. Waiting for Abby to bring the Elk Creeks, I study the walls: *Phi Delts suck. Betas suck. Fijis rule. Ann loves David. David loves Chris. Kilroy was here.*

Holding two Elk Creeks, Abby makes her way down the aisle. On Fridays, she works the evening shift in the Books and Camera department at Miller and Paine, and we like to stop for a drink beforehand. She's responsible; she has just the one drink, enough for a buzz so modest that none of the few customers who visit the department would even notice. Our drinking buddies eventually filter in, get their own Elk Creeks, and come back to our table: Paddy, Smitty, Westy.

Jason's not with them, at least not yet. I look at Abby. She looks at me. She says, "Good."

"Good what?" Westy asks. As far as we know, the other boys don't have any idea what Jason does. We wonder if Jason has told them about us—*easy lays*—a description that perhaps Jason believes himself. Years later, I'll hear that some of the drinking buddies found out what Jason had been doing, and their response was, in many ways, like ours: they still ran around with him, they were still friends, but behind his back they called him a son-of-a-bitch.

"Good drinks," I say.

"Good afternoon," Abby says.

The mood in Sandy's grows jovial and boisterous. By now, the bar is standing room only. Gus, one of the locals, walks around emptying ashtrays into a brown paper bag. He does little chores like that for free drinks.

Outside the window, snow falls. Workers from downtown office buildings and department stores—lawyers, administrative assistants, sales clerks—walk past on the wide sidewalk, heads ducked down against the flakes, hands shoved deeply in coat pockets. How serious they all look, how preoccupied. How can they pass Sandy's and not want to come inside, into the warm, smoky air, loud with laughter? How could they not want to be us? They don't glance in the window to see how much fun we're having. Even when Westy pounds on the glass and yells, "Hello there!" they don't look up from the slick sidewalk, their own feet moving steadily toward whatever they have to do next.

It's as if Sandy's has already been torn down, and all of us standing just feet away from the sidewalk are ghosts, invisible.

Jason's still not here. It's still a good afternoon.

Chapter 11 :: **Omaha, 1985**

The room in Omaha where the preliminary hearing was held was dim and small, with rows of seats for spectators and two tables in the front, one for the prosecution and one for the defense. The judge's bench rose against the far wall.

Joe Griffin sat next to his attorney at the defense table. He wore an orange jumpsuit, and cuffs shackled his ankles together. My parents and I sat in chairs a few rows behind the defense table. I wondered if Joe Griffin could feel my gaze boring into the back of his neck. I hoped he was conscious of how starkly his situation contrasted with my own; I found it deeply satisfying that I sat in a chair I'd chosen, that I wore my own clothing, that if I wanted to get up at any point and step into the lobby for a drink of water, I could. I was, in short, free to do whatever I wanted, and he couldn't take a step without the company of a guard.

Diane was the first witness to testify.

On November 16, 1984, around 7:30 in the evening, she'd been walking home from the grocery store. Daylight savings time had ended, so the sky had turned dark by then. She lived in the same neighborhood I did, and, listening to her testimony, I figured she'd gone to Schaeffer's, the grocery store half a block from Jasper's, where my parents had bought me a whole cartful of groceries when I first moved to Omaha. She'd probably walked past my apartment on her way home. She might even have glanced up at the lit window in the living room as one of us moved past it inside and momentarily blocked the light.

Diane walked down the short alleyway that led to her apartment, and a man ran up, grabbed her, and held a knife against her throat. She described the knife as being similar to one in her own kitchen that she used for slicing roasts. A big knife, a commonplace knife, I thought. Joe Griffin might have taken it from his own kitchen in the house on Lafayette Avenue.

Diane said the man had asked for money. She didn't have much, since she'd spent most of it at the grocery store. He told her to put the sack down and walk across the street with him. He said if she screamed, he'd just run away, but he'd hurt her before he left, so she'd better keep quiet.

Across the street, he took her behind a secluded garage and told her to remove her clothes. Frightened of the knife, she complied. He told her to lie down on the leafy ground. I could imagine the leaves slipping under her feet, the scent they gave off when crushed under her weight. The man attempted penetration but was unsuccessful. He requested oral sex, but Diane testified that she couldn't do it; she was "real sick to my stomach." Eventually the man managed penetration, and after he was finished, he told her she had to stay where she was for ten minutes. "Now I'm going to be watching, and you better not leave within the next ten minutes," he said, because he'd come back and hurt her if she moved before the ten minutes were up.

And how could you know if he was watching or not? His demand to wait might have been simply his chance to get away, to get some distance between himself and the girl he'd attacked. Or he might have told her to wait just to see if she'd do it, if he'd scared her into acquiescence. He might have liked toying with people that way.

Griffin's attorney was younger than Ivory and seemed, I thought, nervous. Later, after I was in law school, I'd understand that the position of public defender was not a desirable job: low pay, too much work, the clientele often the kind of people you did't necessarily want to associate with. The attorney's name was Mr. Regan, pronounced like the President's. He asked questions to clarify what the attacker had been wearing, what the knife looked like, whether Diane had seen the person she believed to be the attacker since the incident occurred.

She thought she might have. She worked at a plasma donation center, and after Joe Griffin had been arrested, she looked through the donor records to see if a man by that name had been in since she'd been attacked.

As a matter of fact, a man named Joe Griffin had sold plasma at the center, but Diane didn't think she'd actually seen him there, even though the time he'd come in had overlapped with one of her shifts. (What if she'd been the technician to draw his blood, I thought. What if she'd had to touch his skin?) Diane said she'd begun making a list of people who might have been the attacker but eventually stopped, since she felt a little foolish playing detective.

The defense attorney moved on to ask about the physical appearance of the man who had raped her. He went over the length of hair, clothing, height. The questioning struck me as informational rather than adversarial. I understood that the defense attorney was in a complicated position; it was 1985, not 1950, and in this particular situation—where the victim had been approached by a stranger, threatened with a knife, and had immediately reported the crime—the attorney couldn't come across as hostile or dismissive. He couldn't suggest that Diane was asking for what happened as she'd been walking home with a sack of groceries. He could only poke at her description, looking for—but not finding—a place he could suggest that the details she related pointed to another perpetrator.

I made note of the defense attorney's strategy.

Tara followed Diane on the witness stand. She held her hands clenched in her lap as she began to tell her story, and she spoke so softly that the judge had to ask her to speak up. "Sorry," she said, and started again. On the evening of December 7, 1984—about a month after Diane had been assaulted—Tara had been with a couple of her friends at an apartment near 42nd and Dodge. She asked if one of them would come with her to the 7-Eleven on Dodge Street so she could get a can of pop and a candy bar. The friend said no, so Tara headed off alone. It was about 11:45. On the way back from the convenience store, a man grabbed her from behind. He held a knife in his left hand, and he told her not to scream.

Tara said, "I wanted someone to hear me so I could get away, so I screamed."

After she screamed, the man cut her stomach with the knife.

He took her behind a pine tree and demanded money. They were by the Clarkson Hospital sign at 42nd and Dodge Street, and he pulled her into an alley. He took her behind some stairs and demanded oral sex. Tara said she didn't know how to do that; she told him she was only fourteen years old (she was actually eighteen at the time). He described what he wanted, she said, and then told her to do it for five minutes.

"Two minutes," she responded, and he agreed.

She had a lot of spunk, I thought. She saw things as negotiable: She'd screamed after he'd told her not to (and gotten cut, which indicated he was serious about using the knife, it wasn't just a prop). She'd bartered about the oral sex and he'd agreed. Was there something about Joe N. Griffin that kept Tara from taking him seriously, something that I had missed? Or was there something about Joe N. Griffin that Tara had missed? Maybe she'd grown up in an environment where threats of violence were commonplace but ultimately idle. But Joe N. Griffin had cut her when she'd screamed after he told her not to.

I thought about the girl Ivory had mentioned, the one who'd been stabbed and left for dead. I wondered again why he stabbed her. Right after Ivory had told me what had happened, I'd imagined her situation through the lens of my own perspective, as a passive girl who'd gotten stabbed even after she cooperated. But maybe she'd been even bolder than Tara. Maybe she'd called him names, threatened to get a family member to come after him and make him pay. And he'd stabbed her to keep her quiet.

My own behavior—obliviously walking down the alley—led me into trouble. But my passivity might also have saved me from something worse.

The problem with Tara's testimony was that she hadn't gotten much of a look at the knife. Before he raped her, she'd asked him to put the knife away, and he had.

Meanwhile, her friends had grown worried when she hadn't come back from the 7-Eleven. They drove around, looking for her, and they pulled into the parking lot near the alley where the rapist had dragged Tara. The idling car filled with people made the attacker nervous enough to let Tara go. She ran to her friends, who took her to the hospital.

None of her friends saw the rapist, and Tara herself hadn't seen him since the incident until the lineup at the beginning of March.

And then my turn to testify arrived. I stood, wiped my palms on my skirt, and walked to the front of the courtroom. I put my hand on the Bible. I swore to tell the truth.

Sitting in the witness chair, I glanced at the defense attorney, who appeared to be only a couple of years older than I was. Joe Griffin glared at me across the defense table. I looked right into his eyes—the most frightening part was actually making myself do it—and then moved my gaze in a leisurely fashion over to Ivory and smiled.

Ivory asked about the evening of February 20, 1985, and I explained how I'd been walking over to Jim's condo when a man called out to me. I made sure to mention that he'd been standing under the streetlight behind Convenient Food Mart. I said I hadn't run when he called to me because it might look rude. Then I told about the knife, the light on the side of the condo building, how I'd tried to get away after he dragged me behind the garage, that I'd been afraid he might kill me.

In the spectators' chairs, my father's posture was the same one he adopted in church during the sermon: head lowered, eyes focused on his hands, which were folded in his lap. My mother seemed to be looking at a point over my left shoulder.

"Thank you," Ivory said. "Your witness," he told the defense attorney.

Mr. Regan wanted to know whether the ground was muddy behind the garage. I said it was. He asked, "Is it fair to conclude that the attacker also would have gotten pretty muddy?"

I pointed out that I'd been the one directly on the ground, getting pressed into the mud, not the attacker.

Next Mr. Regan asked about the attacker's facial hair and clothing, and I provided detailed descriptions of the rapist's stubble, the heavy coat he wore, the pants that weren't made of denim but some other heavy fabric. Some of the questions puzzled me—the one about the mud, for instance; how was the possibility of the rapist getting muddy relevant to the accuracy of my identification of him?—and I considered the defense attorney the enemy, an extension of Joe N. Griffin. I let that show a little when Mr. Regan said, "Did he have glasses on?"

"Yes," I said. "He did."

"What kind of glasses?" Mr. Regan asked.

I looked him in the eye. "Like yours," I said.

A second passed before he responded. "Not sunglasses?"

"No," I said. I pointed at Regan's glasses as I described what the attacker's had looked like. "They didn't droop down quite as far, they were a little more square at the bottom, and there was either a crack in the lens or they were bifocals. I saw like a line in the glasses."

Ivory, who'd grinned when I compared the attacker's glasses to Regan's, spoke up. "Your Honor, let the record show she has described wire-rimmed, teardrop, standard pilot glasses, clear."

The judge said, "So shown, with a crack in the lens."

Mr. Regan asked next about the scarf, whether it was pulled up around the attacker's face. "No," I said. "I remember the scarf because the fringe was hitting me." Regan moved on to what the men in the lineup had been wearing: Was it the same dark cap and glasses?

No, I told him. The cap used in the lineup had been light blue, "but I recognized him even without that on."

Regan asked for some clarification: Had I been in Jasper's, or had the attacker, or both of us? I thought I could see where he was going with that question: He was implying that I'd met Griffin earlier in the evening, in a *bar*, where I'd probably been *drinking*. I explained that the attacker had been standing outside Jasper's and had seen me leave my apartment. Finally, Regan asked, "Now, your identification of, or your certainty in the line-up, was that because of his nose or mouth, what was it?"

I said, "I knew I would recognize that man when I saw him again."

"So, it's not anything specific, just general . . ."

"I remembered what he looked like."

"Just a general recall of everything altogether?"

"Correct," I said.

Regan had no further questions. Ivory had no redirect.

Regan moved to dismiss the charges against Joe N. Griffin. The request struck me as ludicrous; we three witnesses had offered, I thought, convincing testimony that the defense attorney had done nothing to rebut. The judge overruled the motion. He found probable cause and announced the defendant would be bound over to district court for trial.

I thought about the word *bound*, how it could mean both restrained and running free—as a deer across a field. I preferred to imagine Joe N. Griffin bound in sheets, like a mummy, waiting for his trial that would, Ivory explained as we all walked toward the door, take place in the summer, several months away. "These things take some time to work their way through the system," he said. "But you don't need to worry—he'll be in jail the whole time."

I nodded.

"I'll be in touch," Ivory said.

"All right," I said.

My parents and I left the courthouse. The wind had dropped off, and the sun blazed down, but the air still held a wintery bite. On the sidewalk, my father paused. He possessed a deep aversion to conflict—a tendency I'd inherited, though I didn't understand it at the time—always seeking to skirt any sort of confrontation or social or emotional discomfort. Now, he looked to the west, shading his eyes. "There—" he pointed. "That way is the Killian Hotel."

The Killian Hotel, the place his grandfather Johnny Killian had owned. I remembered the story about Johnny Killian tossing the drunk customer out the door.

I squinted in the direction my father was pointing.

"Right there."

Omaha's skyline wasn't familiar to me, like Lincoln's; Omaha's was more crowded with structures, and I didn't know any of their names. This morning the sky was too bright to distinguish individual buildings. My eyes watered from staring into the sun.

"See it?" my father asked, still pointing.

"Yes," I lied.

Chapter 12 :: Lincoln, 1980s and Before

But Lincoln isn't coming across the way I want it to. Acknowledging the sexual coercion and all the drinking makes it sound like a dangerous— or at least unpleasant—place, populated with bored young adults flirting with the same alcoholic tendencies they observed disdainfully in their elders. But that's only an undercurrent that somehow never undermined our capacity for believing that we, like the city of Lincoln itself, were safe and special.

Scott Fitzgerald said, "The test of a first-rate intelligence is the ability to hold two opposing ideas in mind at the same time and still retain the ability to function."

This notion connects to the idea of cognitive dissonance, a theory that focuses on how humans strive for internal consistency. When we experience inconsistency, that is, dissonance—Lincoln is a safe place/Lincoln is not a safe place—we become psychologically uncomfortable. We attempt to reduce this dissonance. We create stories to explain it away, to make the dissonance into an exception rather than a rule, to put it in its place so as to sustain our belief in a more comforting, overarching, narrative.

But why, I wonder, should all of Lincoln subscribe so readily to the same narrative? Clearly not every person in Lincoln shares the same experience. My *we* tends to assume, I suppose, the people I knew in high school and college, people I believed had to be thinking that Lincoln was a special place, that we were safe and special people.

Where did this notion of significance start?

Maybe it began back in the 1860s, when Lincoln—a small village at the time—wrestled the designation of Nebraska's capitol from Omaha. One version of the narrative is that Lincoln was chosen as the capitol because it was more centrally located and therefore more accessible to citizens in western Nebraska. There's truth to this story: Lincoln is west of Omaha by sixty miles, and the population at the time didn't extend to the far western part of the state, hundreds of miles away in Nebraska's Panhandle. The alternate version, the version that Lincolnites favor, involves a marker of some sort—a stone, I remember my father telling me—that was supposed to be the cornerstone of the yet-unbuilt capitol building itself. The city in possession of this stone would be the capitol. Under the cover of darkness, a group of Lincolnites rode their horses to Omaha, where this stone was located. The Lincolnites managed to acquire the stone (Omahans will say "stole the stone," while those of us in Lincoln will say, "took what was rightfully ours") and brought it home. Thus, Lincoln became the seat of government, the location of the main branch of the state university, the place we called "the Star City," in reference to the fact that on maps, a star marked the capitol city while the other, lesser cities were identified with commonplace dots.

That notion of Lincoln's distinction also seemed to be connected in some ways to the department stores that were built in the early years of the twentieth century, at the time Lincoln—now the official capitol of the state—was growing from a village into a proper city. In 1923, the Lincoln

Chamber of Commerce financed the publication of a booklet that extolled Lincoln's virtues. The booklet opens with "The Lincoln Creed," which was identified as "The Athenian Oath Revised," and reads thus:

> We will never bring disgrace to this, our city, by any act of dishonesty or cowardice, nor ever desert our suffering comrades in the ranks; we will fight for the ideals and sacred things of the city, both alone and with man; we will serve and obey the city's laws and do our best to incite a like respect and reverence in those above us who are prone to annul or to set them at naught; we will strive unceasingly to quicken the public's sense of civic duty; thus in all these ways, we will transmit this city not less, but greater, better and more beautiful than it was transmitted to us.

The language of creed—which was, after all, a piece of Chamber of Commerce strategy in a publication that would describe, in breathless detail, every store operating at the time—does contain some clues about the origination of the contemporary Lincoln mentality. There's the *we*, for one thing, uniting Lincoln's citizens in common purpose. There's the rooting of Lincoln's destiny, its perpetual distinctiveness and beauty, in lawfulness and civil obedience. What citizen wouldn't subscribe to such a creed, and once subscribing, not feel secure in such a city?

I can read the booklet and consciously acknowledge that its prose is exaggerated, its ideas hyperbolic, the descriptions of the department stores bordering on the florid. At the same time, I think, well, it's also kind of true.

This same civic pride permeates the contemporary public consciousness. One of my classmates in graduate school, who'd grown up in Chicago, called Lincoln the most self-referential place he'd ever been. The pridefulness wasn't individual; we weren't, on the whole, vain people. But every comment about another city's advantages would be countered with something equally remarkable you could find right here in Lincoln. For instance, mention the magnificent sight of cherry trees blooming in Washington, DC, and a Lincolnite will nod and say, "But have you been to the Sunken Gardens?" The Sunken Gardens is a public park on the corner of 27th and Capitol Parkway, where terraced beds bloom with flowers and the shallow rectangular pools are filled with lily pads and goldfish the size of carp that break the surface of the water and kiss the air. And what's especially distinctive and amazing about the Sunken Gardens, a Lincolnite will tell you, is that it was created on what was the town's original garbage dump. Look how we have managed to transform ugliness into something breathtaking and beautiful, and make note of our resourcefulness!

Some of us express genuine befuddlement at the idea of people wanting to live in New York City, a place considered huge, dirty, full of rudeness and horrific crimes.

Argue that there's so much culture in New York, the art museums and theaters and the universities like Columbia where you can attend readings and lectures open to the public.

The Lincolnite will listen to your argument—we are, after all, noted for our politeness—but his face will be blank. He's unconvinced, and he's waiting for you to finish talking so he can make his point: We have art museums here. And theaters. And the University of Nebraska is here. The University of Nebraska hosts readings and lectures open to the public. Furthermore, people aren't getting shot on the streets.

And then the Lincolnite will play his trump card: What about football? What about Columbia University's football team?

What can anyone say in defense of Columbia University's football team?

The Lincolnite will be too polite to point out that between 1983 and 1988, the Columbia Lions lost forty-four games in a row, still a record number of consecutive losses. But the introduction of football allows the Lincolnite to mention that the University of Nebraska Cornhuskers are five-time national football champions. He'll note the fact that Nebraska holds its own record when it comes to college football: every home game since 1962 has been sold out. That's more than fifty years of sold-out football games. No other school in the country comes even close.

And we have our safe streets and our beautiful parks, our miles of bike trails—paved-over railroad tracks that run through the city—where, on warm Saturday afternoons, joggers run, and safely-helmeted families take leisurely bicycle rides as rollerbladers glide around them.

Because violence is so rare in Lincoln, so intermittent, it startles us when it happens, it forces us to stop and reconsider everything we've told ourselves about our town, what makes us special, what sets us apart. We examine the episodes of violence and create a collective memory—essentially agreed-upon versions or explanations—that smooth out uncomfortable details so that the stories of damage and death lose some of their horror.

Take Charlie Starkweather, for instance, the spree killer who terrorized Lincoln for a week during the winter of 1958. (The Starkweather killings inspired several movies, including *Badlands* and *Natural Born Killers*, as well as the Bruce Springsteen album *Nebraska*.) Every time I drive past the intersection of 24th and Van Dorn, I think of Starkweather breaking into the Wards' house—which was a few lots south of the intersection—forcing the maid to make pancakes, breaking the black poodle's back with the butt of his shotgun, stealing the Wards' car, evading authorities, heading west toward Wyoming. He was eventually captured, tried, and sentenced to death in the electric chair.

The case is solved, closed. But long-time Lincoln residents remember, of course, and share details of that cold winter of 1958, those days when Starkweather roamed the town evading the authorities, and fear gripped the city. Fathers with shotguns patrolling neighborhoods after dark, children sent home from school early, the doors of houses locked, windows locked, anxious phone calls where news and rumors were exchanged. My mother knew the woman who'd been Charlie Starkweather's kindergarten teacher, and she repeats what the teacher told her: Charlie Starkweather had been a *very strange* little boy.

But Starkweather's murder spree has become a story, a morbid kind of touchstone; enough time has passed that it's lost its power to shock. We've found ways to rationalize the incident—an aberration, an exception, however grisly, of violence that proves the rule of safety. So I think of Starkweather momentarily as I pass the intersection of 24th and Van Dorn and then I'm past the block and climbing up the Van Dorn Street hill and thinking of something else.

•

I remember a night in 1988. Early spring. A couple of my buddies from high school and I were driving around with a friend of a friend, a guy who was originally from Oklahoma City. The Oklahoma guy had come to visit his friend, and we were showing him around town. We'd been at a wedding reception; everyone was pleasantly buzzed, and we'd driven through downtown Lincoln, pointing out bars we liked and sharing their distinctive characteristics (*That's Sandy's, where you can write on the walls!*). We followed Cotner Boulevard through Piedmont, a neighborhood of nice, mid-century-modern-ish homes. We drove the whole length of Sheridan Boulevard, slowing in front of houses of people we knew, telling stories about the people and the houses.

A girl I went to college with lived there.

That's where one of my mother's friends lived. She was so inexperienced at cooking that the first meal she made for her husband after they were married was a TV dinner—and she didn't realize you were supposed to take the meal out of the box before you put it in the oven!

That house has a bowling alley in the basement. Just one lane. But it's cool.

That's the old Weaver house. Mrs. Weaver strangled her daughter there in 1972.

A little discussion ensued over the daughter's name: Rhonda? Or Elizabeth?

Juliette said, "She would've been in my sister's class if she'd had gone to Irving, but she went to Pound."

"That's right," I said. The girl had gone to Pound, but she was enough older than I was that I'd still been in grade school when she died. Her younger brother, however, was our age, and we were in Spanish together at Pound. I remembered knowing that his sister had been killed by his mother, and thinking that all the surviving siblings would become morbid and strange—the way you'd expect characters in a horror story to behave—but Ben had always seemed like an entirely normal guy: funny, smart, popular.

The Oklahoma guy was good-looking, good-natured, and he seemed to be enjoying himself. We were stopped at the light on 27th and Sheridan when he turned to Juliette. "This is great!" he said. "This place, it's a small town just like you see in the movies!"

Of course the connection between Lincoln and movies sounded accurate, but his comment about Lincoln being a small town struck me as so strange that I was speechless. Small town? We'd driven him all over the city.

"You know our state capitol is one of the Seven Wonders of the World," I told him.

Juliette looked at me. "Really? I've never heard that."

In the years after I'd learned this fact from my father, I'd stumbled over a couple of lists of the Seven Wonders of the World. Some included the Great Wall of China and Stonehenge; others had the statue of Zeus at Olympia and a pyramid in Egypt. Because of the discrepancies among the lists, I told myself—when none of them made note of the Nebraska state capitol—that I was simply looking at a wrong version of the Seven Wonders of the World.

"My dad said so," I replied, vigorously certain of myself.

"Well," she said, and smiled, accepting the fact and the point it proved: we were special, and not as small-town as the Oklahoma guy had thought.

Chapter 13 :: **Lincoln, 1992**

In the weeks after Candice Harms's disappearance, a somberness prevailed on the UNL campus. So many connections existed: people knew Candice Harms, or knew someone who'd known her, or had gone to the same high school she had. The fact that Candice Harms was a freshman inspired fear in the first-year students. That she was a female inspired fear in many of the women.

At the end of September, authorities planned their seventh search. On horseback, the sheriff's deputies and volunteers combed, once again, the land near the area where Candice Harms's Corsica had been found. So far, the only suspect remained the boyfriend, Todd Sears, who was questioned again and again. He'd had nothing to do with her disappearance, he insisted. The last time he'd seen her was when she'd left his apartment around 11:40 p.m. He was as distraught as anyone.

The suspicion about the boyfriend had a rational basis: statistically speaking, there's a much greater chance that a woman has been victimized by someone she knows, rather than by a stranger. For instance, according to a Bureau of Justice Statistics report on homicide trends in the United States from 1980 to 2008, in 88 percent of cases with a female victim, she knew the perpetrator, either intimately—spouse/boyfriend, or peripherally—neighbor/employer. In only 12 percent of the cases was the perpetrator a stranger.

I wondered what would have happened to Jim if, that night in Omaha, I'd vanished like Candice Harms. If he'd been so absorbed in his studies that he didn't check on me right away, would the police have believed he'd had nothing to do with it?

I felt bad for the boyfriend. If he was innocent.

The UNL Women's Center sponsored a walk and candlelight vigil. The walk followed part of the route Harms normally took when she left her boyfriend's house to drive home. The Lincoln *Journal* ran a picture of five female students grouped together, grim-faced, their long hair in the spiral perms and teased bangs that were the fashion that year. One of the students said, "You expect this kind of thing to happen in New York or Chicago, but not Nebraska. The scary thing is that there's no reason for it to happen. You think, 'It could be me next.'"

I taught two composition classes that semester. The first one met at 8:30 in the morning. Almost all the students were true freshmen; this semester was their first in college. Waiting for class to begin, they sat reading the *Daily Nebraskan*, which contained an article about Candice Harms nearly every day. Or they talked quietly together, sometimes about inconsequential things, sometimes about the missing girl. "Maybe she ran away," Sarah said. "Maybe she ran away to . . . ." She looked at the girl next to her for help. "Brazil," the other girl said. "Brazil," Sarah said. They were both silent for a moment, as if imagining Candice Harms in an exotic South American landscape, wearing sunglasses, smiling as a harmless, handsome man approached and held out his hand.

One of the boys said, "I bet the boyfriend had something to do with it. They should check the dump."

Did he know something? I wondered. He was a strange kid; he liked to come up while I was packing my books after class and talk about himself, things he was reading, interesting events of his life, plays he'd been in during high school. He wore the sort of clothes I associated with drama geeks—the pinstripe vest from a Salvation Army suit; a skinny necktie with his wrinkled, short-sleeved shirt; a porkpie hat. He stood a little too close when he talked, and his mode of discourse tended toward monologue rather than conversation. I had ten minutes between the end of this class and the beginning of the second class, and occasionally he'd follow me down the hall, still talking.

Eventually, he turned his attention toward Sarah and trailed her out of the room after class was over. Maybe he didn't bug her the way he bugged me, I thought.

Or maybe she was just being polite in the way Nebraska kids tend to be polite, afraid of confrontation, afraid to look the strange boy in the eye and say, "Get lost."

In a normal semester, the strange boy's behavior would have seemed simply irritating rather than borderline ominous, but since the disappearance of Candice Harms, we saw omens and suspicious activity everywhere. Simple coincidence became something darker, like the knife I found in the parking lot one Tuesday evening at the beginning of October when Yogi and I walked to the car after night class.

I was with another woman in the graduate program, who was describing an occasion when she'd felt menaced. One night, years earlier, she'd awakened to a flashlight shining through her bedroom window and into her face. She'd told this story before; she had been deeply affected by it, but she seemed to expect a level of horror or outrage on the part of the listener than was greater than I felt the incident deserved. She'd been terrified, and I could understand that, but no one had choked her, or held a knife to her face and told her to take off her jeans.

But I didn't bring up these details. My classmate and I were merely acquaintances, not friends. She wasn't someone I could see myself confiding in; shortly after we'd first met, she'd told me she thought I was *male-identified*, which at the time meant the sort of woman who required male affirmation to confirm her existence. I asked what I did to give her this impression. "You wear lipstick," she said.

Half-listening to my classmate's story of the man and the flashlight, I looked down, and right in front of my feet lay a hunting knife enclosed in a leather sheath. "Wait," I said. I pointed at the knife, and we stared at it silently. I knew we were both thinking the same, illogical thing, that the knife had something to do with Candice Harms's disappearance. But of course it didn't; already weeks had passed since she'd vanished, and the knife was in a spot where it would have either been run over by a car or found by someone else if it had been lying there any length of time. Chances were that it belonged to a student who'd come to Lincoln from western Nebraska and went around with the knife tucked in his belt, because a knife was a necessary tool in that area—you might need to cut aside overgrowth or splice a wire or skin an animal you'd shot for food. And, earlier this evening when the knife's owner had been climbing into his pickup truck parked in the lot we were crossing, the knife had fallen out.

I picked up the knife and slipped it out of the casing. Wooden handle, a five-inch blade that had been sharpened and was scratched from use. The metal glinted in the light from the streetlamp on the edge of the lot.

"Should I leave it?" I asked.

"I don't know."

I could put it back on the ground for the boy who'd dropped it to find when he came looking.

But if he didn't come back, someone else might pick up the knife, someone with malicious intent, who might be walking on campus at this very moment. I didn't want to leave it for someone like that to find.

I tucked the knife in my purse and took it home.

•

Did I need to do something about the student I'd come to think of as Strange Boy? I wondered, watching him pursue Sarah out the door. Did a teacher have an obligation to manage the way her students behaved after class was over? I couldn't imagine any of my own professors telling one of the dull graduate students to quit talking to a disinterested fellow student.

As the days passed, I noticed that the students had taken care of the issue themselves. At the end of class, Sarah zipped up her backpack, slowly, while Troy and Dan came around the table. Strange Boy stood next to Sarah, talking, talking, talking. The group of them moved out the door, Troy in front of Sarah and Dan stepping behind her, in between Sarah and

Strange Boy. You could walk three abreast down the halls of Andrews, but there wasn't enough room to walk in a line of four, so Strange Boy found himself either in front of or behind the other students, who had begun their own conversation.

In a normal semester, I might have felt a little sorry for Strange Boy, the way his social ineptitude made the other students shut him out. But now I was simply relieved. His pushy behavior needed to be curbed, and I was glad to see the students take the initiative themselves so that I didn't feel compelled to intervene.

And his comment about checking the dump—that didn't mean he knew anything special. A lot of people were saying to check the dump, which was less than six miles from where Candice Harms's car had been found on Bluff Road.

Perhaps the authorities had already been there, holding the sleeves of their jackets against their noses and mouths to muffle the stench as they combed through acres of trash, the garbage a spongy thick layer that sank under their feet. Crushed cans glinting in sunlight, discarded car parts oxidizing orange with rust, an occasional valuable among the refuse, like an heirloom knife that had been carelessly dropped into the trash when somebody scraped plates after Thanksgiving dinner. There was garbage at the dump, and treasure, and perhaps even a body that had settled down through layers of coffee grounds and egg shells, shredded bills and wadded paper, and into the arms of one of the old Miller and Paine mannequins, whose own fingers had been broken off, blind painted eyes staring at nothing.

•

By 1992, most of the old familiar grocery stores were gone. Binger's had become the Towne Center Showroom, a place that sold hot tubs. An office supply warehouse occupied the Hinky Dinky building. Safeway was now Dot Drug.

But Ideal Grocery was still Ideal Grocery, and many of the clerks I remembered from childhood still worked there. The twins who'd reminded me of the Smothers Brothers—now in their fifties—stood behind cash registers or wheeled customers' groceries out to the cars. Yogi and I passed Ideal every afternoon on our walks. Often one of the twins would be in front of the store, and he always waved.

Candice Harms's face still looked out from the flyers attached to light posts, but the ink had started to fade, the tape that held the corners in place curling and coming loose.

In my house on California Court, I kept moving the knife I'd found in the parking lot. I couldn't decide where it belonged in my things: It wasn't like someone's serving spoon, innocently appropriated after a potluck that you filed in your silverware drawer with other spoons before you returned it. The knife was a hunting knife, a weapon, and I didn't own any other weapons I could store it with.

For a couple of weeks, I left the knife sitting on the kitchen counter. Then I moved it to the coffee table in the living room, next to the ashtray, and stared at it while I smoked. I thought about the knife Joe N. Griffin had held in front of my face that night in 1985, seven years earlier. Was it true that every seven years all the cells in your body replaced themselves so that periodically you were, in some ways, a totally different person?

Whatever cellular turnover had occurred, no replaced cells had taken my memory of that night with them.

But over the years I'd refined the story of it so that it fit into a familiar narrative, the cautionary tale. Its moral? That the rape had taught me a valuable lesson about being careful, that it had given me something I could use.

But was I careful? I made assertions like, "I never walk alone after dark," but this assertion was untrue. Even in the fall of 1992, before Candice Harms disappeared, I walked alone to my car after night class ended. I could have joined the other students in their plans to walk together, but I'd had an aversion to ingratiating myself into the group and mapping out plans: *We'll all walk to Leslie's car, and then she can drive us to the parking lot by the health center, and Betsy can drive Molly home.*

Why had I avoided joining in, I wondered, looking at the knife.

I hadn't wanted to be one of those paranoid women who saw the world as a place filled with danger. I wanted to maintain my perception of myself as all in all a lucky girl—and Lincoln as an essentially predictable place. Perhaps I was even relying on a statistical rationale: I'd been attacked once, so what were the chances of it happening again?

But then I wondered if something even stranger was going on, connected to the possibility that in a small way I continued to blame myself for my assault. I'd been oblivious, reckless, stupid. Did I, in some deeply

buried part of my brain, think I deserved the punishment of being attacked again? Was I tempting fate?

And was that why, for the most part, I kept the rape to myself? Wouldn't
sharing the information invite wide censure or judgment about my behavior, both past and present?

There were other reasons for not telling. The language of *survivor* and
victim bothered me in a way I had trouble articulating. Years later, I would
read an article in the *New York Times* by Parul Sehgal that explored the
complications of the victim/survivor terminology. Entitled "The Forced
Heroism of the Survivor," it opened with a discussion of the sexual molestation Virginia Woolf experienced at the hands of her half-brothers.
Writing about this abuse, Woolf noted, "It is so difficult to give any ac-
count of the person to whom things happen." What words do you use to
situate yourself in the experience? That was the trouble I had with *victim*
and *survivor*. How could I talk about being raped without putting myself
in one of those categories?

Sehgal's article articulates the trouble I had—my own aversion—to
those reductive terms:

> In Japanese, the word "trauma" is expressed with a combination of
> two characters: "outside" and "injury." Trauma is a visible wound—
> suffering we can see—but it is also suffering made public, calcified
> into identity and, inevitably, simplified. Perhaps there was some la-
> tent wisdom in Woolf's ungainly little phrase: "the person to whom
> things happen." It's roomy and doesn't pin you down at any stage of
> suffering or recovery. It centers the person and not the event—which
> is crucial. Those who have faced sexual violence are so commonly
> sentimentalized or stigmatized, cast as uniquely heroic or uniquely
> broken. Everything can be projected upon them, it seems—every-
> thing but the powers and vulnerabilities of ordinary personhood.

I didn't want the assault to control how I thought of myself and my
place in the world. If asked to describe who I was, my instinctive reply
would be, "I'm a Lincoln girl." That, I thought, should explain the way I
was, passive, trained in politeness, nostalgic, and admittedly sentimental
about the past. The rape was a "thing that had happened." It did not control who I was.

But in the fall of 1992, I knew only I didn't want to align myself with either of those reductive categories any more than I wanted to join the little group of graduate students who planned how they'd get to their cars after night class, making sure none of them would be alone in the darkness. Their behavior implied the sort of dangerous undercurrent in Lincoln that I denied, and made a point of publicly denying by walking to my own car alone.

Too, I thought that people might view me differently if they knew what happened. It would affect my identity; I would become *the girl who was raped*, just as Ben Weaver had become *the boy whose mother murdered his sister*. But I had more control than he'd had over how widely my story was known. If people didn't know, I could maintain the illusion, not that it hadn't happened, but that it hadn't *changed* me. I controlled the story of my life by omitting a significant element: I remained a certain type of character in the narrative—the invulnerable, resilient girl who strolled through the familiar streets of her safe hometown, sifting through layers of memory, entertained by almost everything she saw, because she understood the links between buildings and people, buildings and the past, contemporary people and their ancestors. The town itself was like a story, continually revealing connections. If I stayed here my whole life, I thought, eventually I'd understand everything about the city.

When I did tell anyone about the rape, it tended to be a boy, and I tended to be drunk. In the aftermath of the attack, I'd found it easy enough to talk to the cops and my attorney Ivory about what had happened. They wanted the facts, where I'd been standing, what the attacker had been wearing. They took notes on what I said. I was comfortable with this objective, business-like approach, which I came to associate with the way men responded to the assault. I had been exceedingly uncomfortable talking to the rape crisis counselor. She wanted to discuss feelings, to connect with me emotionally. The only hope I had for holding myself distinct from the clichéd rape victim/survivor was not to succumb to emotion. That would allow the rape to exert undue control over how I lived the rest of my life.

Outside, the boards of the porch creaked as Yogi stood up and walked over to his water bowl. I took the knife out of the sheath. Examining its scratched, sharp blade, I realized it was a tool as well as a weapon. A tool should join the screwdriver, hammer, and pliers in the toolbox I kept in one of the kitchen cupboards. I stubbed out my cigarette, took the knife in the kitchen, and put it inside the toolbox, which I shoved back on its shelf. I could hear my grandfather saying *a place for everything, everything in its place.*

The knife was out of sight. I could stop thinking about it.

Chapter 14 :: **Omaha, 1985**

Abby and I shared the apartment on Farnam Street in Omaha with three other girls. One, Susie, was Abby's classmate in pharmacy school, and the others were high school friends of Susie's from Fremont. The apartment was officially a two-bedroom; Susie and Abby each had one of the real bedrooms, and Judy slept in a little sun porch on the second floor. Tracy curtained off the dining room for her bedroom, and I occupied the unfinished basement. This space was on the grim side: cement floor, cinder-block walls painted pale aqua, one small window set next to the ceiling. I wasn't there much—when I wasn't at work, I spent most of my time at

Jim's condo—but it didn't seem quite fair that I paid the same amount of rent as Susie, who had a nice real bedroom right down the hall from the bathroom.

There were some other things about Susie, too. We kept our food on particular shelves in the pantry and in the fridge. Every time I opened my jar of Jiff, the remaining amount of peanut butter appeared significantly less than what I'd remembered. Abby said she'd come in the kitchen once and caught Susie holding a jar of Jiff—*my* jar of Jiff—and digging a spoon into it. Susie herself never bought peanut butter because she said it was fattening.

Abby's yogurts disappeared from the fridge, too. The food thefts and disproportionate bedrooms were small issues; a larger one was that I was creeped out by the fact that the rapist knew where I lived. He was locked up, yes, but what if he had friends who decided to get revenge? They'd know exactly where to find me.

So when it came time to renew the lease at the beginning of June, Abby and I decided to move on. We found a place about a block away on Harney Street, in a group of row houses. Every house had one upper and one lower apartment, each with its own entrance. We rented an upper-level apartment in the middle of the row. This apartment was considerably smaller than the one on Farnam Street, but the rent was only $190 a month, and the apartment had hardwood floors, two bedrooms, and old-fashioned hexagonal tiles in the bathroom. Big windows in the kitchen and living room let in plenty of light. There was a semi-finished attic we could use for storage.

We broke the news to Susie, who yelled and then sequestered herself in her bedroom with a six-pack of generic beer while we removed our things. Abby and I lugged our mattresses down Farnam to 40th Street, where we stood, sweating, and waited for the light to change. Then we hauled them up the slight incline of 40th, turned right on Harney, and made our way to the new apartment. We loaded chairs into Jim's station wagon and piled kitchen equipment and bags of clothes into our own cars and drove them over. Carrying a heavy box of books up the stairs, I momentarily regretted that we hadn't chosen a ground-floor apartment.

Abby, who was handy, put new fabric on the cushions of our living room chairs, so everything matched. We unrolled an Oriental-looking rug from K-Mart on the floor. We hooked up the stereo and blasted REM while we unloaded our food—now safe from Susie—into the refrigerator and cupboards.

The window in my new bedroom looked out over the parking lot behind the apartments, and I could see Jasper's as well, there on the corner of 40th and Farnam. If I let myself, I could picture Joe N. Griffin standing outside the bar on that strangely warm evening in February, smoking a cigarette that he flicked away when he heard the door of the old apartment swing open. But I preferred not to indulge that memory. It was better to draw the curtains and turn away.

•

After Abby and I had moved into our new apartment on Harney Street, I told my mother I wanted a dog for protection. What I had in mind was something menacing; ideally, a Shar-Pei—I loved their exoticism, their wrinkled skin and droopy jowls—but I'd settle for a Rottweiler, or a German shepherd, or a Doberman pincher. On a chilly day in June, Mother called from Lincoln and said she had located a dog.

"Good," I said. "What kind?"

"A pug," she said. "She's eight years old, and if you don't take her, she's going to be put to sleep." Mother explained that the dog, Missy, belonged to a young couple who was divorcing. The husband didn't want the dog, and the wife had moved to an apartment that didn't allow pets. The apartment Abby and I had rented didn't allow pets, either—that is, there was an official "no pets" clause in the lease—but you could see cats sunning themselves in the front windows when you walked past, and the manager himself, a corpulent and somewhat creepy man with a patch over one eye, acknowledged that he didn't enforce the clause unless the animal caused problems.

Mother knew the wife's parents—they'd played bridge together for years—and they told her that Missy was a wonderful little dog. Their daughter had spent months searching for someone to take her. No one wanted an eight-year-old Chinese pug, and so the daughter was considering euthanasia. "Unless," Mother repeated, "you're willing to give her a home."

"But I want a dog for protection," I said. "How big is she, anyway?"

"She's not that big," my mother said. "But she's a Chinese dog, like Shar-Peis are Chinese dogs, and she's wrinkled, like a Shar-Pei, so she's just about what you're looking for. And besides—"

I didn't want to hear the euthanasia argument again. "All right," I said, unenthusiastically. "I'll take her."

"And it doesn't matter how big she is," Mother continued. "People never know what a dog might do."

•

Missy spent a couple of days with my parents in Lincoln, and then they brought her to Omaha on a Friday, one of my days off. I opened the front door and looked down at a wheat-colored dog with a smashed face, black ears, and a wildly wagging tail. Her tongue hung out the left side of her mouth. She was making strange snorting noises, like she was growling or choking.

"What's wrong with her?" I asked.

"That's how they sound," Mother said, briskly.

The dog raised one of her front legs and pawed the air as if she was waving. Her mouth hung open in what looked like a maniacal grin. She seemed so delighted to see me that I felt myself warming up, if only incrementally. "Well, come in," I said.

Missy danced into the apartment. I unhooked her leash and she hauled herself up the stairs, all the while making those growling/choking sounds. "It's just the way she breathes," Mother said. When Missy got to the top of the stairs, she stood in the hallway and looked down at me. Her curled tail swung from side to side. She lifted her paw again and waved.

"She is pretty cute," I said, grudgingly.

By the time my parents left, half an hour later, Missy's good-natured disposition had completely won me over. Having always been a cat person, I wasn't experienced in dog care, but I wanted to show Missy that she was welcome, so I shared my lunch with her, pouring out her own small cup of soup with a few bites of biscuit on the side. She loved the soup. I found some dried beef in the cupboard and fed her three slices. She loved the dried beef, too. I filled up a bowl with regular dog food—a whole can of Mighty Dog—and she ate that, snorting in enjoyment and wagging her tail. Shortly after Missy finished the Mighty Dog, she threw up, and I felt terrible: I'd wanted her to feel welcomed, and instead I'd made her sick.

Abby and I had talked about Missy before her arrival, and we'd decided that she'd be *our* dog, that we'd share her. With this in mind, I put a dog bed in the hallway between our two bedrooms. Within days of her arrival, however, it was clear Missy was going to be mine. She never slept in the dog bed. She either slept in my bed with me or, when I stayed at Jim's, which I did most nights, she slept on an overstuffed chair in his bedroom.

After he'd gotten used to the snorting, Jim was captivated by Missy, so much that he'd stop at our apartment on his way home from school—while I was at work—and take her back to his condo so they could spend the evening together. He'd lie on his stomach on the bed, studying, and Missy would lie next to him, resting one paw on the page of the book he was reading to help him keep his place.

•

The trial of the *State of Nebraska v. Joe N. Griffin* was scheduled to begin at the end of June 1985. I met with Ivory before the trial started, and he explained how he'd present the evidence, the order in which the three of us—me, Diane, Tara—would testify. Since Tara was the most nervous of the witnesses, he'd have Diane go first, then Tara, then finish with me. He expected the entire trial would take two or three days, so I should plan on testifying on the last day.

We were sitting in his office in the Hall of Justice building, smoking. After we discussed the upcoming legal proceedings, I found myself telling him about Missy. She was so delightful I couldn't keep from talking about her almost constantly, relating the number of people who'd stopped to pet her on the morning walk, or some charming new behavior she'd exhibited. Because I hold Missy on my lap when I smoke, I told Ivory, she'd begun racing up to me, tail wagging, whenever I picked up my pack of Virginia Slims Lights. *I'm* READY, she seemed to be saying.

Ivory laughed. "She sounds like a good dog," he said.

I asked what other cases he was prosecuting. He began telling me about one of the most recent ones, which involved a couple who had given their baby a bath in water so hot that the child suffered third-degree burns. Cook the kid, Ivory said, and claim it was a mistake, that you didn't know how hot the water was. He shook his head in disgust and flicked his cigarette against the side of the battered metal ashtray on his desk. "People and their fucking problems," he said, "I tell you."

People and their fucking problems. I loved the phrase the minute I heard it. I immediately recognized how it could fit almost any situation—an irate customer calling Ramada, a doofus ahead of you in line at Hinky Dinky, a snotty sales clerk. When I got home that afternoon, I shared the phrase with Abby, and we both found plenty of opportunities to use it.

I still say *People and their fucking problems*, and every time I do, I think of Ivory, even though he's been dead for years.

•

The trial began on Friday, July 19, 1985. Ivory scheduled my testimony for Monday the 22nd. He told me that I couldn't sit in on the other girls' testimony, and that we weren't supposed to talk to each other about the trial until we'd all testified. Allowing a witness to hear other witnesses' testimonies prior to her own might influence what she said and compromise the defendant's right to a fair trial. After you'd testified, of course, you could watch the rest of the proceedings.

Diane, Tara, and I had all heard each other's stories at the preliminary hearing, so this restriction struck me as somewhat moot. As a matter of fact, Regan—Griffin's attorney at the preliminary hearing—could have requested that the witnesses be sequestered, but he might not have thought of that; it was, after all, his first case.

I was intrigued by these rules and strategies. Law was a field of study I'd never considered pursuing, but my experience with the legal system had made me curious about how the whole process worked. Did I want to go to law school? I wasn't sure.

On Friday evening, Abby and I sat in the apartment on Harney Street with Lloyd Cole on the stereo, drinking Bud Light and painting our nails while we speculated about what might have happened that day at the trial. After the polish dried, we leashed up Missy and walked over to Convenient Food Mart to pick up more beer.

It was around seven thirty; the sky overhead had taken on the washed-out blue color it acquired between daylight and dusk. We walked past Jasper's, past our old apartment. All the other girls we'd lived with had moved out by then, and the place was starting to look a little run down. Trash tangled in the bushes by the deck and the drawn shades gave the apartment a shuttered appearance, like the people inside were doing things they didn't want you to see.

We moved to the other side of the street at the spot where I'd crossed the night I'd been attacked. Did it seem strange that I'd remained in the neighborhood and traced the same path I walked that night? I had, of course, made changes in my behavior: For one, I never wandered outside alone after dark. At night I drove to Jim's condo instead of walking, and he would be waiting for me at the top of the steps that led down to his unit. Ultimately, staying in the neighborhood was less of a conscious choice to reclaim the space than a practical matter. The pharmacy school was only two blocks from our apartment, and Abby needed to live close to school. We were roommates and best friends. I never even considered getting a place of my own in a different neighborhood.

When we arrived at Convenient Food Mart, Abby asked, "Do you want to get the beer or stay outside?"

"I'm fine," I said. "I'll stay with Missy."

Abby went inside the store. In the weeks and months after the assault, I'd found myself adopting certain behaviors that allowed me to feel safe, or at least not menaced: I accepted my mother's notion that "people never know what a dog will do," so I took Missy with me whenever I walked somewhere. I didn't maintain any illusions of her as an attack dog—she was, perhaps, the friendliest animal I'd ever met—but I figured she'd bark if pressed.

I also performed a mathematical assessment whenever men approached. A lone man was more dangerous than two apparently unconnected men. Who knew what the lone man's intentions might be? Yet even if he were inclined to attack a woman, surely the proximity of another man would deter him.

Two men together made me uneasy. If I saw two men walking toward me, I crossed the street.

In front of Convenient Food Mart, I stood in the middle of the parking lot, in full view of the store's plate glass windows. I watched cars passing on Farnam. If one had turned into the lot, I would have moved to a spot a safe distance away. I didn't think of myself as paranoid, simply cautious. Cautious, and fine. Recovered. Ready to testify against the rapist in three days.

Abby returned with the beer. We'd started toward home when I saw Diane and another girl coming toward us on 39th Street. "Hey!" I called.

Diane waved.

"I got a dog!" I said, a little louder than I'd intended; Abby and I had already polished off a six-pack back at the apartment. "You've got to meet her!"

"Okay."

Missy approached Diane, who was wearing sandals, and licked her toes, then looked up, tail wagging. Diane laughed. Her friend, a serious-looking girl with short hair, smiled.

I knew we weren't supposed to talk about the trial. But we hadn't sought each other out to collude. We'd simply run into each other, both of us walking the same streets where our paths had crossed that of Joe N. Griffin. An accidental encounter.

I said, "How's it going?"

Diane shrugged. "All right. I'm glad it's over."

"Did Tara do okay?"

"She did okay," Diane said. "She was pretty mad when she talked about what happened."

Missy sat down beside me. Abby and Diane's friend were standing back a little, Abby holding the sack of beer tucked under her arm. I thought how odd it was that the randomness of violent crime had given me common ground with a girl I probably otherwise never would have met. Overhead, the sky had grown darker. Streetlights blinked on.

Diane said, "You're going on Monday?"

I nodded. I'd already ironed the dress I would wear, and I imagined briefly telling the story again, this time in front of a jury, of how I'd been walking over to Jim's condo, eating an apple, when someone called out to me. I'd turned to see a man standing under a streetlight. I'd experienced that rush of instinct that told me to run, instinct I'd ignored.

Diane and I made eye contact. I felt a sense of tension in the air around us, created from my own desire to ask about the defense attorney's strategy and her desire to tell me. But we were good girls, we knew we weren't supposed to be talking to each other at all.

I said, "Tell me."

She lowered her voice. "It's the lighting thing again. Whether we could accurately identify the guy in the dark."

The same tactic the lawyer had used at the preliminary hearing. "Okay," I said.

On the night of the attack, I'd walked across this exact spot of sidewalk where Diane and I now stood. By then, Joe N. Griffin was already following me, maybe still deciding what he was going to do, waiting to see if I went into Convenient Food Mart. Or maybe he'd already decided by that point. He'd already told himself, *when she goes down that alley, I'll call out to her.*

"Good luck," Diane said. She leaned down and gave Missy a little pet on the head, and then she and her friend started across the parking lot, cutting toward Farnam Street.

Her friend turned back for a second. "Cute dog," she called.

Chapter 15 :: **Lincoln, 1982 and 1992**

I read that our perception of objects is based not only on what we observe but what we remember. So, for instance, if you see any part of a dog behind a fence, your brain assembles the whole dog—because you've seen dogs before and remember what they look like—even though you only actually see the visible parts of the animal.

I can't remember when I first noticed the abandoned building on the south side of O Street, directly across from the old railroad depot that had been repurposed as a branch of Union Bank and Trust. Chances are I was in high school, which was when I'd developed an interest in alleys and what passed for squalor in Lincoln. While I loved walking past the carefully tended yards on Sheridan Boulevard, there was something about decay—the possibility of surprise, an untold story behind abandoned objects and boarded windows—that piqued my curiosity. In the alley behind the old creamery building on 8th and P, for instance, I once saw a stack of claw-footed bathtubs, nestled inside each other like teacups.

Where had they come from? What would become of them? The alley itself was brick—likely the original brick that had been laid down back when Lincoln was first developed. I stood for a moment, studying the bathtubs, contemplating the mystery of their presence.

The abandoned building on O Street was three stories tall, long and narrow, with a façade of crumbling off-white stucco. Two windows flanked a door that opened to the main floor. One window was boarded up with faded plywood. In the other hung a sign: For Rent or Lease/Front Main Floor/Upper 2-Floors/Parking Lot.

Driving down O Street with my father, I asked, "What was that building?"

"It was a cathouse," he replied, and explained that prostitutes had worked there to accommodate the railroad workers. Its official name was the Midtown Hotel, and a bar called Johnny's Tavern occupied the ground floor.

I saw that some of the upper floor windows had been broken out. Shredded window shades hung above the remaining shards of glass.

What was the appeal? The bathtubs, Johnny's Tavern seemed to be whispering secrets to me, secrets of other lives lived here, the town's past, hidden connections I'd be able to see if I simply looked long and hard enough.

I'd had this compulsion to look for connections and create stories as long as I could remember. Staring out the window at Elliott, the school of the mean boys, I wondered about the houses they lived in; the smell of their unwashed clothing reminded me of the odor of places I'd gone trick or treating, where piles of newspapers leaned against the walls and the carpet underfoot crunched with dirt. The mean boys probably lived in houses like that. I could put pieces of what I knew together with imagined pieces and create a story. I could explain things in a way that made sense. And it did, I suppose, give me a sense of power, turning a person into a character and stepping into his mind, figuring him out, cutting him down to size.

And so Johnny's Tavern became a little project that I investigated for years, peering in the front window every time I walked past or looking at the upper stories when, driving, I had the good fortune to be stopped by a traffic light in the right place. Johnny's was located in the no-man's-land of O Street. The main shopping area, which ran from 10th and O up to around 15th, contained the department stores, like Miller and Paine and Gold's, and smaller specialty shops, like Stephenson School Supply, Hospe's Music, Sartor Hamon Jewelers. Once you got east of 16th, O was lined with car lots, auto repair shops, second-hand stores, places that sold extremely specialized items that were of no interest to me, such as plumbing supplies, trophies and ribbons, and a couple of bars, the Spigot and the Lodge, that Abby and I had never visited because they catered primarily to local alcoholics.

One late December night in 1982, after last call at Sandy's, my boyfriend and I went over to the Midtown Hotel to look around. Snow piled at the edges of the sidewalks. A stiff wind blew from the east.

I peered in the front window of Johnny's. Of course it was too dark to see anything, but I'd looked inside so many times that I knew its contents: an expanse of empty floor, a bar along the back wall. An emptiness that sometimes gave up clues in the daylight, like the time the sun was in exactly the right spot to hit a glass sitting on the bar and reveal its presence.

My boyfriend walked around the building. His father owned a sporting goods store located in the main shopping area of downtown, with their last name scrolled across the store's façade.

At the time, neither of us had any idea how close downtown Lincoln was to changing. We had no idea that 1983 would mark the beginning of the end of the downtown we'd known all our lives, the familiar stores shuttered, one by one, beginning with Gold's. Eighteen years later, the family's sporting goods store would be closed, the name taken down, all evidence of the building's original purpose erased when someone opened a bar there. I went inside only once and stood, unsettled, in the dimly lit area where bicycles had once been displayed. The bar was located where the checkout counter had been. Someone flung open the glass door and staggered outside to vomit on the tile between the entrance and the sidewalk.

But that was all in the future, the faraway, unimaginable future. My boyfriend and I looked up at the broken windows of Johnny's Tavern, the sign above the door that said On and Off Sale Beer, which meant you could drink beer inside the tavern or buy containers of beer to take away, and Entertainment Nightly. In the dark, you could barely make out the art deco designs on the upper façade.

Five months later, in May 1983, Johnny's would be torn down. The Lincoln *Journal* ran a picture of the building on the day before the demolition began. "The notorious Midtown Hotel building at 20th and O Streets is being demolished," the article said. "Because of its proximity to the Rock Island Railroad tracks, the hotel was known for years as 'Ma Kelly's,' a house of ill repute. In recent years, it had been a rooming house—eventually closed by city officials for health code violations—and a refuge for transients. Lincoln investor William Spader, who bought the property in 1977, said plans for the site are uncertain at this point."

But, in December 1982, the building had been sitting in its present decrepit condition for so long that I believed it would stay there, in that way, forever. I would have all the time in the world to continue my investigation of Johnny's Tavern. Peering in the window, I wondered: What had happened on the last night Johnny's was open? Who'd been the last person to exit the bar and lock the door? And what did the upper floors look like? I pictured little rooms with plaster walls and wood floors, hooks on the walls for clothing, some old mattresses with blue and white striped ticking that had been left behind.

And who was Johnny?

I could imagine something about Johnny, too: a short man—like my great-grandpa Killian, whom I'd never met but knew from my father's story about him tossing a drunk out of his hotel. Perhaps Johnny was still alive, perhaps he still lived in Lincoln and sometimes drove down O Street, past the bar he'd owned, feeling a rush of nostalgia for the nights the place had been full, the patrons drinking, toasting each other, laughing. The place one large party—the way Friday afternoons and Wednesday nights at Sandy's Bar were one large party we were sure would never end—and Johnny himself the host.

A condemned notice had been stapled to the wood of the boarded-over front window. "Do not enter," it warned. "Under the order of the building inspector of the city of Lincoln. Unsafe to occupy."

I rattled the handle of the front door, which was, of course, locked. What would have happened if the bolt had magically slipped and the door swung open? I would have seen this occurrence as miraculous, an invitation from the universe to step inside. *Unsafe* would have had nothing to do with me.

•

Sometimes a memory can be strong enough to allow you to see what is no longer there.

In college, Abby and I spent many weekend nights at the Drumstick, a bar on North 48th Street in Lincoln. My mother told me that the one-story stone building had once been a dentist's office, but we knew it only as a place operated as a restaurant during the day, serving fried chicken; on weekend nights, the Drumstick hosted bands on a stage set up in front of the big picture window that looked out on 48th Street. One night, the story went, Nick Lowe had taken a cordless microphone out into the middle of 48th Street and sang "Cruel to be Kind" while cars whizzed around him and the Drumstick's patrons stood in the parking lot, watching. My college boyfriend had been there and swore the incident was true.

By 1992, the Drumstick had been torn down. But if I didn't look at what replaced it, if I didn't even glance at that side of the street when I drove by, I could still feel the building's presence, and a lurch of memory was strong enough to pull back a particular night in all its specifics, as if I'd truly traveled back in time:

It's the end of May 1982. Abby and I head toward the Drumstick as the sun is beginning to set. Tonight REM is playing. The cover charge is $5.00 in advance, $6.00 at the door. We arrive early enough to score a table right on the edge of the dance floor, under one of the chandeliers made of wagon wheels. We order cans of Budweiser.

Eventually our drinking buddies show up, the guys we've known since high school, where they were a class or two ahead of us. We've all been going to the same bars and parties for years, and the relationships Abby and I have with these guys are both superficial and intimate. We've slept with some of them, kissed others, know about their DWIs and who their girlfriends are and what kind of cars they drive. We recognize certain shirts, can identify particular boys by their smell: Polo cologne, or Drakkar Noir, or Dial soap. Most of the boys have nicknames: Westy and overall-wearing Jethro (after the character on the Beverly Hillbillies) and Jimbo and Paddy.

Jason, the boy we know we need to avoid at parties, is there, too. Talking to him is safe at the Drumstick. The activity of the Drumstick—the band

and dancing—is engaging enough that no one wants to miss it, so Jason doesn't bother trying to talk girls into going outside with him to sit in the car and hear about his troubles with his girlfriend.

The sky is fully dark when REM comes onstage. Cigarette smoke swirls in the light from the wagon-wheel chandeliers. The band plays one great song after another—"Radio Free Europe," followed by "So. Central Rain" and "Elysian Fields" and "Talk about the Passion"—so we dance, non-stop, for hours, until our clothes are wringing wet with sweat. Everyone is cheerfully drunk. Finally, the band leaves the stage. The waitress refuses to bring us any more beer. The bouncers force us outside at 1 a.m. and lock the doors behind us. "Go home!" one of them yells, his voice muffled by glass.

Moths flutter around the streetlights on the edge of the parking lot. Car doors slam. Tires slide in the gravel of the lot's surface as vehicles pull out onto 48th Street. Those leaving in cars turn left out of the lot, headed toward Vine Street, because everyone at the Drumstick knows you'd have to be crazy to drive down heavily patrolled O Street after a night at the bar. The cops are thick on O Street, pulling over gearhead teenagers racing their souped-up cars and the drinkers who don't know the town the way we know the town and don't understand the routes that allow you to move under the radar.

Someone inside shuts off the lighted Drumstick sign. In five years, the Drumstick will be sold, torn down, replaced by a McDonald's. We have no idea this unthinkable event lies in the future, as we linger in the night air, laughing and flirting, waiting to see what will happen next.

•

Because something would happen, surely. Something magical or at least funny—we'd hook up with one of the boys or someone would know of a party or maybe a couple of people would come over to the house I shared with Abby, and we'd stay up late drinking beer and talking. We were accustomed to chance encounters leading to interesting situations. We *expected* these chance encounters; leaving the house to do something as mundane as grocery shopping, I'd feel a little kiss of anticipation along my nerves. Who might we run into?

We never thought we'd run into someone dangerous, someone we didn't know who had mischief or worse on his mind. But by 1992, I had to acknowledge that possibility existed. It changed the way I felt as I walked or drove through the town, because I knew now that a person can never understand everything she should about the place she lived. I could see buildings that no longer existed, but beneath the vibrant ghosts of the past, I could discern a knot of menace that now pervaded Lincoln, one that seemed to have started with the disappearance of Candice Harms. The identity of the perpetrator or perpetrators remained a mystery. Who were they, and were they here among us?

Chapter 16 :: **Lincoln, 1992**

When Candice Harms drove through the intersection of 48th and Vine—a block north of where the Drumstick had been—Scott Barney and Roger Bjorklund were behind her. By then, the men had been driving around for hours, looking for a target. Sometimes when you're not getting your way—when things don't seem to be falling into place—you decide to give up. You decide that whatever you want isn't meant to be. Barney and Bjorklund weren't those sort of men. The longer they searched for a lone woman to abduct and assault, the more fully committed they became to their plan. They had the materials they needed, and they were owed, they believed, this thing they wanted to do.

They first saw Candice when she stopped at the light at 27th and Vine on her way home from her boyfriend's. They tailed her down Vine Street, along the side of Gateway Shopping Mall, and followed her as she pulled into the Chateau Le Fleur's parking lot. It was almost midnight by then. The lot itself was quiet, the apartment complex dark. No one stood outside taking the air or smoking a cigarette on his patio. Candice Harms parked her Corsica, and Barney pulled in behind her.

"Now," Barney said.

Bjorklund got out of the car. He left the door open so the sound of the police scanner they had—the dispatcher's voice, the little fizzes of static—would be audible to the girl. Bjorklund walked up to the driver's side door and told Candice Harms he was a cop. He held up his gun as proof.

She asked what she'd done.

They'd discuss that when they got to the station. It was a serious matter, serious enough that he was going to have to confiscate her car; he'd drive and his partner would lead them downtown.

He pushed her onto the passenger seat. The books she'd left sitting there fell on the floorboard. Candice Harms must have been shaken that a cop would be so rough.

Driving, he held the gun on her. His job now was to keep her from jumping out of the vehicle, to keep her persuaded that he was, in fact, police, and that she'd be fine if she cooperated.

No one can know what was going through Candice Harms's mind on this drive along the quiet streets. She was a Lincoln girl, an "all-around good kid," according to her mother, so chances are she possessed that same streak of politeness and passivity I saw in my students at the university and that I possessed myself. She'd grown up in this town, and she might have held the same assumptions I held, that danger was something that happened in other cities. If someone said he was police, he must be police—why would someone lie about that?

Did they pass any cars on Vine Street as they headed west? Did they stop at red lights as Bjorklund drove away from, rather than toward, downtown, where the police station was located?

How can we begin to imagine what is happening inside the Corsica, the conflicting thoughts going through the girl's mind? The notion of Lincoln's safety colliding with the evidence of its danger; the man with gun who was not, as he'd initially claimed, a police officer. Perhaps Bjorklund offered the reassurance that if she cooperated, they'd let her go. Perhaps he held the gun on her the whole time they drove and said he'd shoot her if she moved. How can we imagine the paralyzing disbelief at what is happening here, on a school night toward the end of September when most of the town's focus is on the upcoming football game against Arizona State?

The caravan of two went north, toward Bluff Road, through a construction zone, to the spot where Bjorklund parked the Corsica next to the field of milo.

Out there in the country, late at night, no one was around to see what they were doing. No one heard her when she screamed. The fields gave off the smell of the decaying remains of the harvest. In the distance, semis rolled along the interstate.

Barney bound her hands with rope and wrapped her head in duct tape.

The men put the bound girl in Barney's car. Bjorklund returned to the Corsica to retrieve Harms's purse, and he locked the passenger side door. The air had grown cooler, but it was still a beautiful night. And now they had accomplished the first part of their plan.

•

Five arterial streets run north to south through Lincoln: 27th, 48th, 56th, 70th, 84th. In 1992, 84th Street marked the eastern edge of the city.

At the intersection of 84th and Havelock, signs of habitation exist. On the southwest side sits the L-shaped compound of the Lincoln Agronomy Farm Headquarters: five dun-colored metal buildings and a silver silo. A grain elevator rises on the northwest corner, kitty corner from the Lancaster Event Center, where Lancaster County holds its annual fair. The northeast corner is a cornfield.

Two blocks east of the intersection of 84th and Havelock Avenue, the pavement on Havelock ends, and the road turns to gravel right before you cross the bridge over Stevens Creek. Trees line the creek's banks, and a trail runs just west of the bridge, perpendicular to the road, and leads into the trees. Kids in the area go out there to drink beer.

We had our own spots like that on the south side of town. Weekends, somebody'd load a keg into the back of his car, and we'd all drive into one of the fields on the outskirts of the city. We didn't know who owned the fields; they seemed abandoned, and we didn't think we could be hurting anything, just a group of us gathered around a bonfire, drinking beer, laughing, flirting.

Who drives on Havelock east of 84th Street? People who live out in the country. People who still farm, or who want some land around their house for horses, or people who like the quiet you get that far from the center of town. Those are the sorts of people who are home and in bed at a reasonable hour. They're not driving east on Havelock at one a.m. on September 23, when Roger Bjorklund and Scott Barney arrive with Candice Harms in the back seat of Barney's car, her hands bound, her face wrapped with duct tape. The car bounces from the gravel road onto the trail that leads into the trees.

By the end of September, the harvest is over. The cornstalks are dead but still standing, their dried-out leaves rattling in the breeze, a sound like ghostly applause. Candice Harms might hear the sound when the men remove the tape from her head after they take her out of the car. Bjorklund and Barney know there's no one around to hear her screams, here where the town turns to farmland, traffic at this hour on 84th Street so intermittent as to be nonexistent.

These men had planned carefully. They knew how the city worked.

Roger Bjorklund stands outside with Candice. Scott Barney gets back in the vehicle. They're low on gas from all that driving around they did, looking for a victim. He drives into town to refill the tank.

Back at 86th and Havelock, on the ground by Stevens Creek, Rodger Bjorklund is raping Candice Harms.

Barney returns. He gets out of the car. The girl is on the ground, her clothes disordered. Barney rapes her while Bjorklund watches.

They've now completed their fantasy: They abducted this girl. They raped her. What will they do next? They could take her back to her car on Bluff Road, drop her off with a warning not to go to the police. She has doubtlessly seen both their faces well enough to put together composites. She might have heard them call each other by name. She must've seen the car Barney drove when he pulled up behind her Corsica out on Bluff Road, before the men wrapped her head in duct tape. She has come to know details that might lead to their arrests if they let her go. And she has a horrifying story to tell, being fooled into thinking that Bjorklund was police, then the abduction, the rape by not just one of the men but both of them.

And these men are worried about getting caught. The reason for them deciding against robbing a bank tonight was, after all, that they'd had an intimation they'd be apprehended. So they'd forgone the robbery in favor of this fantasy. They'd spent hours discussing the plan, refining the details. Later, after they were arrested, their description of the fantasy—their acknowledgment of what they'd intended to do—always stopped with the abduction and rape. They never said their fantasy included murder. Admitting that murder was part of the fantasy suggested premeditation. Though Bjorklund would eventually refer to himself as a "dumb follower," these men weren't stupid. They'd had plenty of time to iron out all the details as they cruised the streets of Lincoln.

Now they stand by the banks of Stevens Creek in the middle of the night, the girl they'd brutalized lying on the ground.

In the end, each will blame the other for what happens next.

Chapter 17 :: Omaha, 1985

On Monday, July 22, 1985, the day I testified in the trial of *Nebraska v. Joe N. Griffin*, I wore a Kathryn Conover dress of printed floral fabric—green and turquoise leaves, interspersed with little salmon-colored blossoms—that had long sleeves and a peplum at the waist. White shoes with modest heels. I had a couple of these outfits, pretty summer dresses with matching shoes, to wear to weddings.

The trial took place in a different courtroom than the one where the preliminary hearing had been held. This room was much larger. Benches for spectators lined two of the walls, and the judge's bench rose at the front of the room. The witness stand was located between the judge's bench and the jury box. My parents had driven up from Lincoln, and they sat facing the witness stand. Sunlight shone through the long windows and filled the room with light.

The jury consisted of ten women and two men. I sat up straight in the witness chair, with my feet together and my hands folded in my lap. Joe Griffin was at the defense table with his attorney, wearing a suit: the clothing of a normal, innocent person. Even though I refused to make eye contact with him, I could feel him glaring in my direction. I knotted my fingers in my lap to hide their shaking.

Ivory established that I lived in Omaha, and then said, "So you were going to see your fiancé on the night of February 20th, is that correct?"

For a second, I was surprised that he'd made a mistake; he knew Jim and I weren't engaged. But then I understood why he'd said what he did. The tests done on my underwear had revealed the presence of two blood types, one of which presumably belonged to the rapist and one that belonged to Jim, since we'd had sex that morning before I'd gone to work. Ivory had to explain away the other blood type.

"Well," I said, glancing down at my ringless finger for a second and then smiling at Ivory, "he's not my fiancé. Yet."

Ivory smiled back: I couldn't have played it better. "All right, then. You were going over to your boyfriend's, correct?"

I told the story, responding to Ivory's questions, my fingers linked together in my lap, my voice calm. Sometimes I looked over at the jury while I talked and made eye contact with one or another of the women. I'd been angry and a little bit mouthy during the preliminary hearing, but I understood that I needed a different persona for the trial. All these people hearing my story had to trust me. They had to think I was a nice girl. And didn't I appear to be a perfectly nice girl, with my pretty cotton dress, my fingernails painted a modest pink, my almost-fiancé boyfriend in medical school? A nice, innocent girl who'd made the mistake of walking down an alley in the dark.

I related the details of the mud, the knife, the choking. One of the women in the jury box covered her lips with her fingers.

Ivory asked if the man who'd assaulted me was in the courtroom. I said yes. "He's right there." I pointed toward the defense table.

"No further questions," Ivory said. He nodded at Griffin's lawyer. "Your witness."

Defense attorney Justin Cooper—a deputy public defender—was

young, though not as young as James Regan, who'd handled the prelimi-
nary hearing. Cooper's questions proceeded as I anticipated they would.
He asked whether I'd really been able to get much of a look at my attacker:
It was fully dark at ten thirty, wasn't it?

"Yes," I said. "But the man who raped me was standing under a streetlight when I first saw him."

"But that was fifty feet away from you?"

"Maybe a little closer than that. And I saw him up close after he'd
grabbed me. There's a security light on the side of the condo, and we were
maybe ten feet away."

"But he grabbed you from behind, correct?"

I hated having to make any sort of concession. I said yes.

"So you didn't see his face, then."

"But I saw him after he'd thrown me on the ground next to the condo."
My palms were damp with sweat. I reminded myself not to slouch, to keep
my shoulders back. "I saw him."

After I'd finished testifying, the judge called for a short recess. Joe Griffin would take the stand after the break.

Ivory said I had to leave the courtroom while Griffin testified. My parents were going to stay and listen, but I needed to leave. "Now, you know,"
he said, pushing open one of the double doors that led to the hallway and
guiding me through, "I don't want you in here because you might stand up
and scream at him when he starts telling his story." He smiled, and his tone
indicated he was joking—of course Ivory knew I wouldn't do something
like that—at the same time he was acknowledging that yes, I did have every right to stand up and scream at Joe Griffin. "You can sit out here and
have a cigarette. You did a great job."

"Okay," I said.

Wooden benches lined the wide hallway, and I found one with an ashtray positioned next to it. The fabric of my dress was sticking to the small
of my back, and when I lit a Virginia Slim, my hands shook. I took a deep
drag on the cigarette and blew smoke at the ceiling.

People walked past. You could guess at the reasons they were in the
courthouse by the clothes they wore: the lawyers in their suits and shined
shoes, carrying briefcases, witnesses in everyday clothes, walking slowly and looking at numbers on doors. Some of the lawyers and witnesses
glanced over at me, as if they were wondering what I was doing here.

I finished my cigarette and began cleaning out my purse, wadding up old receipts and movie ticket stubs and tossing them in the ashtray. I found a blank piece of notebook paper, smoothed it on the bench next to me, and began writing to Abby. Ever since we'd met in high school, we'd been inveterate note writers. In our sociology class at Lincoln Southeast, we spent the entire period passing notes back and forth, filling sheets of paper with comments on the other students' comments, discussions about where we might have lunch, long and detailed descriptions of dates that, had the note been confiscated and read aloud, would have caused us to die of mortification. When we weren't together, we wrote each other letters.

Dearest, I wrote. *I'm sitting outside the courtroom while the rapist testifies. I wonder what he's saying.*

I let myself imagine what was happening behind the closed door to the courtroom: *Joe N. Griffin takes the stand. He swears to tell the truth, so help him God. He sits in the chair where I'd been sitting earlier. Does he prop his elbows against the arms? Has he been coached on how to sit? How to make eye contact with the men, at least, on the jury? Does he clasp his fingers together or let them swing freely?*

I lit another cigarette. I would find out from my parents exactly what Joe N. Griffin testified.

On the stand, he said he didn't remember where he was on November 16, the evening of Diane's assault. "It's just like any other day," he said. He claimed he didn't own a knife. And he couldn't remember what he was doing on December 7, when Tara was raped.

He did remember where he was the night I was attacked, however: he was home watching television with his stepfather and stepbrother. The stepfather testified that Joe Griffin had been wearing a bathrobe and watching television when he himself went to bed around 10 p.m. on the night of February 20.

Deputy Public Defender Justin Cooper asked Griffin, "Do you know of any reason why these three women would identify you as their assailant?"

"Maybe because I look like their assailant or something," Griffin said.

After Griffin's testimony, the defense rested its case. The jury was given instructions, and they retired to deliberate a few minutes before 4:00 p.m. Ivory came out of the courtroom. I stood up. "We're done," he said. "It's in the jury's hands now." He said he would call me the minute he heard the verdict. The minute he heard. He promised.

My parents had followed Ivory into the hallway. I tucked the note I'd been writing to Abby into my purse. "How about some supper?" my father said.

While my parents and I left the courthouse, Griffin was taken back to jail. We crossed Farnam Street and headed toward M's Pub, the oldest restaurant in the Old Market (it had been founded in 1972 and would be destroyed, decades later, by fire in January 2016), where we'd gone for lunch after the preliminary hearing. It was a nicer place than we'd normally patronize, a little more expensive, and I knew that meals there were a treat, a reward, a way my undemonstrative parents could express their concern.

We followed the hostess to a table. In the jail five blocks away, Joe N. Griffin changed out of the regular clothes he'd worn to testify and back into the orange jumpsuit. As we perused our menus, Joe N. Griffin was probably looking around the cell he'd left earlier that day. I imagined him sitting on the edge of the thin mattress, cracking his knuckles, telling himself he'd been convincing, that in a day or two he'd be out, and then he'd come after those girls who'd put him through all this and make them pay.

"Ranch," I said when the waitress asked what kind of dressing for my salad.

And the jury—what was the jury doing right now?

My parents begin relating the testimony they'd heard while I was in the hall, the stepfather and stepbrother saying Joe N. Griffin had been watching television the night I was attacked.

"They're *lying*," I said. "That's *not true*." Since the rape, when I found myself getting angry, my appetite vanished, and I sat staring at the plate the waitress set in front of me.

"Eat your salad," my mother said. My parents had both picked up their forks and held them above their plates, waiting for me to follow suit.

"Would you do that?" I asked my father. "If you knew I'd done something bad, would you lie and say I hadn't done it?"

"Yes," he said.

"You would lie?"

"Yes."

"Why?"

"Because parents are supposed to protect their children."

"But—" I started. I wanted to argue that truth superseded notions of parental duty, that Joe N. Griffin's stepfather was wrong, wrong for lying—his story was, essentially, condemning my story as false. He was suggesting that I was a liar, or at least mistaken, not a good observer.

But my own father would lie to protect me. His statement surprised me, deeply.

"Amy," my mother said, "eat your salad."

"All right." I poked my fork into the lettuce, arranging a small, tidy bite on the tines, the way we'd been taught in White Gloves and Party Manners. The ranch dressing was homemade, tangy with dill, and delicious.

Chapter 18 :: **Lincoln, 1992**

On September 23, 1992, after Roger Bjorklund and Scott Barney raped Candice Harms on the banks of Stevens Creek, they forced her back into Barney's car. They drove ten miles across town to the far southern out-skirts of Lincoln—134th and Yankee Hill Road—and parked beside a field, where a single cottonwood tree stood, shedding its leaves onto the harvested ground.

The girl was dragged from the car. Bjorklund put her in a choke hold to control her and began walking her across the field. Barney followed. In the darkness, on the uneven ground, Bjorklund tripped. He fell on top of Harms, breaking her neck.

She was shot twice in the back of the head as she lay face down in the field. Out there, no one was around to hear the gun go off.

The two men walked back to the car, and then Bjorklund returned to retrieve a blanket they'd left behind. The girl was still alive. He could hear her breathing, making wheezing, choking sounds. Bjorklund thought she was suffering and that she wouldn't survive; he told himself it was inhumane to let her suffer like that.

He then shot her five times with his revolver. He retrieved the blanket and the men left.

They returned to 86th and Havelock Avenue and burned her clothes and the blanket.

They drove east to Pawnee Lake. They threw their guns into the water.

Two days later, they returned to the field at 134th and Yankee Hill Road. By then, articles about Candice Harms's disappearance had appeared in the paper. The police had found her car on Bluff Road. They'd interviewed her parents and Todd Sears. Deputy Tom Casady had asked the public for help. Had anyone seen the girl?

Bjorklund and Barney dug a little grave in the field near the cottonwood tree. Bjorklund rubbed what he described in his statement as "airline fluid" on her skin. He gave no reason for this. Possibly he thought it would cause her body to decompose faster. Then they pushed Harms's body into the shallow hole, and Bjorklund prayed that "God would . . . take her to heaven."

They left the field. For months they moved among us, unbeknownst.

•

The weather in the fall of 1992 remained temperate during the shortening days of October—that is, temperate for Nebraska in October: snowless, with afternoon temperatures in the 40s and 50s. I wore a black leather jacket on the afternoon walks Yogi and I took along the bike trail that curved behind the Children's Zoo. The zoo sat on the west side of the trail and on the east side was Antelope Creek, a narrow stream that you could barely see in the summer when overgrown weeds on the banks obscured the water. Now that the nights had dipped below freezing and killed the foliage, the creek was visible, and it made a faint musical sound when it slid over rocks.

How deep was the creek? I wondered. Probably only a foot or two, but the water wasn't clear enough that you could see the bottom.

By October, some of the Children's Zoo animals had been moved to their winter quarters in the big indoor zoo next door—the building often referred to as the smelly zoo—but the llamas remained in their pen, and they trotted to the fence when we approached.

Candice Harms had been missing for almost a month. The searches of the dump and the fields by Bluff Road turned up nothing. The authorities had no leads.

The students in my composition classes couldn't stop talking about her, repeating the same questions in the conversations they carried on in the moments before class started: How could someone just vanish like that? Who was next? And her parents—oh, her poor parents, how could they bear the mystery of her disappearance, the terrible thoughts that must keep them awake at night?

Walking with Yogi, I thought about that morning's class discussion, which had focused on whether there were any subjects too serious to joke about. Sara (the former object of Creepy Boy's attention) immediately raised her hand. "Disappearances," she said. "Candice Harms."

The rest of the students nodded.

"Illness," another girl, Margaret, said. "Bad luck." She began relating an incident—*a true story*, she emphasized—that had happened to a friend of a friend of hers on the previous year's spring break. Vacationing at Padre Island, this friend of a friend had met a charming, handsome guy—"from Yale, or somewhere like that, he said"—and they'd struck up a romance. They talked of a future together. He said he'd fallen in love. And then, after one last night of passion before they parted to return to their respective schools, the girl woke in bed, alone. She spoke the boy's name, but he was gone. When she went into the bathroom, she saw a horrifying message scrolled in lipstick (*her* lipstick) across the mirror: *Welcome to the world of AIDS!*

Several students gasped. A few of the girls covered their mouths. I asked Margaret if she believed the incident had really happened. She appeared shocked at my question. "Yes," she said. "It's a true story."

Of course the story was one of those urban legends—like tales of ghosts haunting dorms—that crop up on college campuses. It wasn't actually true. Margaret wouldn't be able to locate that friend of a friend to whom the incident supposedly happened. But, like so many urban legends, as a cautionary tale, it held an aspect of truth, a hard kernel of fact in its plot: an innocent victim (that gullible girl), the charming boy whose only goal, his only true motive, was to inflict harm. The tale illustrated how danger could disguise itself, how it was everywhere. That was a lesson we'd all learned this fall.

Even so, I wanted Margaret—I wanted the whole class—to understand that the AIDS story was an urban legend. I pressed: What was the name of the friend's friend? Or the friend?

She folded her arms. "It's a true story," she repeated. Some of the other students were nodding. They wore the expressions they had when I told them something they didn't want to hear: *No, you can't have an extension on your essay; we're having a pop quiz over the reading.*

Why, I wondered, were they so invested in believing this tale—this horrible tale—that hadn't really occurred?

I continued wondering about this as I walked Yogi past Antelope Creek. Was their stubborn insistence so dissimilar to my own persistent perception of Lincoln?

Yogi stopped to sniff at some grass. Directly west of us, behind the fence that separated the Zoo's property from the rest of the park, stood a cage with vines woven through its metal links to lend a more natural, less cage-like appearance. I thought of it as the monkey cage though I hadn't seen a monkey inside it in the year Yogi and I had been taking our walks along the trail. In fact, I hadn't seen any type of creature inside it during this time.

So why was I so certain it was the monkey cage? I recalled an image I'd carried since childhood: a monkey swinging on a bar suspended from the cage's roof.

Maybe the monkeys stayed so close to the ground that I couldn't see them through the vines. Or perhaps they were elsewhere temporarily, for medical treatment or private showings. I could find all kinds of ways to reassure myself that this was still the monkey cage. But I was seeing—as I frequently seemed to be—a Lincoln that was no longer there, layers of the past pulsing beneath concrete evidence of the present. No less stubborn than my students, I preferred to think the monkeys were simply out of sight, sitting on the ground and picking through each other's fur for fleas.

Of course the season was too cold for fleas. Of course this enclosure was no longer in use.

In the end, the situation was of no consequence—what difference did it make? Except, standing there in the chilly afternoon, I began to understand how emblematic this was of the way I experienced Lincoln: expecting things to be a certain way and rationalizing what I saw to make it consistent with what I chose to believe.

Yogi and I continued walking. I looked down at the creek. It was easy to imagine a girl there, like Ophelia in the painting by John Everett Millais, lying on her back in the river, covered with flowers and singing, before she drowns.

•

By Thanksgiving of 1992, the temperate fall weather had been replaced by the expected cold snap. Snow covered the milo fields that bordered Bluff Road; it blew into drifts against the fence posts at the intersection of 84th and Havelock Avenue. The water of Stevens Creek froze over. Snow coated a pile of ash next to the creek that contained unburned metal items: part of a lipstick container, eyelets, a bra hook, a snap, a button, part of a mirror, part of a belt buckle. Snow hid the path that ran parallel to the creek.

A skin of ice thickened on Pawnee Lake, twenty miles west of 84th and Havelock Avenue. Beneath the ice, in the shallow water at the edge of the lake, lay two weapons: a .38 caliber revolver and a .380 caliber semi-automatic pistol and shell casings.

On the far southern outskirts of Lincoln, snow fell on wheat fields, the roofs of barns.

Antelope Creek froze. Snow buried the weeds along the banks. Walking Yogi, I wore a black wool coat, a scarf wrapped across my nose and mouth. The wind that whipped from the south made my eyes tear.

In the house at 610 S. 52nd Street, where Roger Bjorklund was living—alone now, since his wife Shannon had moved out in September—a .38 caliber shell casing lay under the washing machine, undiscovered.

The night before Thanksgiving of 1992, Scott Barney joined his mother and several of her friends from the Goodyear plant for drinks at the Disabled American Veterans Hall on 70th and Seward Street. The DAV's parking lot had been scraped clean of snow. The flags out front snapped in a chilly wind. Inside, the windowless, one-story building was full that evening. A holiday spirit prevailed, and Barney appeared to be in good spirits himself, laughing with his mother, joking with her friends.

The members of the DAV had placed a container on the bar to collect donations for Candice Harms's family. The missing girl's picture was taped to the container. It was the photo used on the billboards, with the red blouse, cream-colored sweater, Candice's lipstick complementing her sweater. Barney exhibited not a bit of strange behavior—not a flinch of guilt, or uneasiness, or any indication he possessed any knowledge about the girl—when he stood right by the donation canister, tapping a folded bill against the wooden counter and waiting to order another round of drinks.

Chapter 19 :: **Lincoln, 1972 and After**

The students' persistence in believing terrible urban legends and my own tendency to impose my safer past upon the present called to mind an incident that had occurred just blocks away from the house on Hillside a few years after we'd moved to the south side of town.

•

May 28, 1972. I'm ten, it's a Sunday, and I'm wearing pantyhose for the first time. I stand on the patio behind our house, holding Emerson, the cat, while my mother snaps a photo. The day is turning warm already, and the pantyhose are proving to be something of a disappointment: I'd imagined they'd feel cool and glamorous against my skin, and instead they are scratchy and hot.

Four blocks away, in one of the big houses that face Sheridan Boulevard, a girl two years older than I am lies dead in her bedroom. At this moment, no one—besides the woman who killed her, the girl's mother—knows.

•

Over the years, fact, speculation, and rumor stewed together to obscure and distort the details of the Weaver murder. People thought they remembered. They thought they could tell you exactly what had transpired, the precise order of events, explicit rationales of motivation. But the story had become its own sort of urban legend, hearsay piled upon hearsay, speculation given the weight of fact. What bits of truth remain in the various tellings of the Weaver murder? Why do people choose to believe one version over another?

I went past the Weaver house on the nights in high school when I couldn't sleep and jogged down Sheridan Boulevard. I drove past the house any time I headed toward Southeast High School or downtown. The house itself was hardly ominous: two stories, grey stucco with white trim around the windows. It sat on a large lot with a tennis court in the backyard. Every time I looked at it, I thought, *a girl* died *there*.

The Weavers were a family of six, the parents and four kids, three boys and a girl. There were two older boys, then Elizabeth, and then Ben, who was in my class in junior high and high school.

The father was a doctor. The mother, whose grandfather had been the publisher of the local paper, was described as a socialite. The children, by all accounts, were good kids: smart, polite, athletic. The Weavers weren't one of those families with a problem child who gets himself addicted to drugs or impregnates someone or drives drunk and causes a fatal car accident.

So you have the façade of the connected family in the lovely house on the desirable street, though the house itself was located on what I called the poor end of Sheridan. On the opposite side of the street, across the island that divided the east- and west-bound lanes of traffic, sat a pair of duplexes. They were nice, well-kept duplexes, with a large shared courtyard of carefully tended lawn, but still: duplexes.

And then things began to go wrong with the Weaver family. After two decades of marriage, the parents split up. In 1970, the mother filed for divorce on the grounds of mental cruelty. The father moved out and re-married the following year. The mother and kids stayed in the house on Sheridan Boulevard. The children went to their same schools; the mother saw her old friends, women she'd known since they were girls growing up in Lincoln.

Then, on the morning of May 28, 1972, the mother got up early and went to church at St. Mark's. She came home. She went upstairs. Elizabeth lay sleeping in her bedroom. Later, the mother would say she opened the door to the girl's bedroom and was confronted with a horrible sight: the girl was on fire—literally burning alive—and so she rushed in, and pushed a pillow over the girl's face, trying to extinguish the flames, trying to save her daughter.

She failed. The girl died.

The autopsy report indicated the girl had been strangled with the tie of a woman's bathrobe.

Psychiatrists examined the mother. They determined she'd suffered hallucinations at the time of the killing. They concluded that she had been in the grasp of "religious delusion" and hadn't intended to kill the girl. The county attorney, Paul Douglass, declined to press charges.

The mother was sent to Menniger's Clinic in Kansas to be treated and was eventually released. The family covered the expense.

The surviving children went to live with the father and his new wife.

The Lutheran Church, which sat directly to the west, eventually pur-chased the Weaver house to use as office space. This struck me as a reason-able sort of use: the house of death had become associated with an insti-tution of faith. Besides, anyone in Lincoln with knowledge of the murder believed that no family in their right minds would want to live there.

•

Those are the facts. Of course details open themselves up to interpreta-tion, and some of these interpretations solidified in people's minds as the truth. Years after Elizabeth Weaver died, people still remembered the in-cident. Some took the story of the girl being on fire at face value. They ac-cepted the hallucination. They believed that the mother had, in fact, been mentally ill, and the girl's death was the result of this illness.

My mother recalled a strange occurrence on the Monday afternoon after Elizabeth's death was reported in the morning paper. The address of the neighbors who lived directly behind us was 4218 Sheridan, exactly four blocks away from the Weaver house at 3818 Sheridan. Our neighbor Marilyn was standing in her front yard, watering the lawn, when she saw a car creeping along the street, pausing as if in search of a house number. The car stopped in front of Marilyn. The occupants stared at her, covering their mouths as if they'd seen the devil. Apparently they'd thought they were in front of the Weavers' house and that Marilyn was Jane Weaver, the mother who'd killed her daughter.

The woman in the car's passenger seat made eye contact with Marilyn. She shook her head, and then the car sped away.

I wonder who those people were. I wonder whether they ever realized their mistake. Perhaps even now, all these years later, they still tell the story to each other—the story they believe to be true: *Yes, the paper reported Jane Weaver had been taken to the police station, but she was actually standing in her front yard, watering the lawn. We saw her.*

•

Some folks didn't buy the hallucination detail. They focused on the cause of the girl's death—that she'd been strangled, rather than smothered. That fact forced you to doubt the mother's story. There were rumors about her involvement with a man who'd broken her heart. (The mother of one of my high school friends told me the name of this man, where he worked, that he had a history of breaking women's hearts. Was any of this true?) Maybe the failed romance had something to do with Elizabeth's death. Elizabeth's murder. And there were other rumors, that the mother had intended to kill all the children, or that she planned to kill three of them and had solicited the help of one of the older boys in this endeavor. The divorce, people said, had turned her malevolent in some tragically Shakespearean way. She'd managed to escape punishment because the family had been well connected, and the county attorney—who had political aspirations—had been so influenced by their connection that he declined to file criminal charges. She got away with murder, some folks muttered darkly.

I always wondered how much of this Ben Weaver heard.

•

By the time Joe N. Griffin came to trial in Omaha, I'd developed an aversion to walking past anyone on the sidewalk. The aversion wasn't close to panic or even anxiety. I'd be walking along, see a person approaching—any person, a woman or a child or an old grandmother pushing a stroller—and find myself deciding to cross to the other side of the street.

The aversion persisted after I moved back to Lincoln to go to graduate school. Even walking along Sheridan Boulevard, which was possibly one of the safest streets in the city, I felt myself stiffen when someone approached. It could be one of the nuns from the Cathedral of the Risen Christ or a person I knew, like the neighbor lady who lived next door; I'd either cross the street entirely or at least move to the grassy island that divided the east and west bound lanes of traffic.

By the time I'd acquired Yogi and bought my house on California Court, the aversion had mostly passed. No one ever approached Yogi without asking permission; in fact, other pedestrians frequently got over to the edge of the sidewalk to avoid us, or sometimes crossed the street themselves.

•

In 2004, thirty-two years after Elizabeth Weaver's death, a For Sale sign appeared in the front yard of the Weaver house. It was a couple of days before Halloween. The listing agent was a friend of my parents, so I called and made an appointment to look at the place. It seemed miraculous to me that I had finally been granted the chance to go inside.

Since the house had been used as office space, there'd been no reason to update the décor. The interior was the same as it had been on the day Elizabeth Weaver died: the same gold and black scrolly wallpaper above the living room fireplace, the same carpet in the first-floor master suite. The stairs that led from the main level to the second floor were narrower than I'd expected.

Upstairs, the realtor followed me as I walked from room to room. Our conversation was desultory; we never broached the topic of the Weaver murder, although I'm confident it was on her mind, the question of how many potential buyers were going through the house—as I was—only because of what happened there.

Two large adjoining rooms on the back of the house with white walls and plain blinds in the windows must have been the boys' rooms. On the east corner was a room with peach-colored walls and matching curtains over the windows, which looked out onto Sheridan Boulevard. Soft carpet covered the floor. This must have been Elizabeth's room, I thought, the place where the girl had been sleeping on that May morning in 1972, when her mother climbed the steps, walked down the hallway, and turned the doorknob.

•

I can see now that the way I reacted to the Weaver murder explains why I avoided, in the years after the attack, talking with people I didn't know well about the rape. What I feared most from strangers was that same attraction to the sensational that I recognized in myself. My own investigation of the Weaver murder—reading newspaper articles; talking to people in town who'd known the Weaver kids or whose parents had known the Weaver parents—turned up distinctly different and often conflicting stories. People—and I admit I was one of them—prodded over the details, speculated, drew conclusions that hardened into fact.

I saw how mistakes and misinterpretations could be made. I saw how they congealed into *the truth*.

I didn't want people to get wrong ideas in their heads about me.

I didn't want the fact of the rape to turn me into a topic of conversation. I didn't want people parsing the details of the assault, questioning, speculating, getting things wrong. I didn't want to imagine what they might be saying:

What did she expect, walking down an alley after dark?
Do you think she's lying?
She should consider herself lucky—at least she wasn't killed.

•

It's so easy to get things wrong. And for what's wrong to solidify into what we become sure is fact. For years I remembered the murdered Weaver daughter's name as Rhonda. I was absolutely certain. When I went to the Bennet Martin library and asked the librarian for help finding newspaper articles on Rhonda Weaver, she tapped on her keyboard and asked if I was sure about the first name. There was nothing on a Rhonda Weaver. There were, however, articles about a murdered Elizabeth Weaver.

Initially, I responded the way the students had when I questioned the veracity of the World of AIDS urban legend. "No," I said, "I'm positive the girl's name was Rhonda."

The librarian was patient, clearly used to dealing with mistaken patrons. Perhaps I wanted to look at the articles on Elizabeth Weaver anyway?

Where did I get the name Rhonda? Who knows. I consider my mistake ultimately fortunate. What more perfect proof did I need of how easily anyone can get something so wrong and hang on to it for dear life? How careful we need to be about even the smallest details if our realities are not to shift into fictions.

•

Standing in Elizabeth Weaver's bedroom, I tried to imagine how the furniture might have been arranged back in 1972. Where had the bed been? Against the hallway wall, or under the window? I stood in front of the window and looked down at the Sheridan Boulevard sidewalk, at the spot where I'd stopped so many times over the years and stared up at the window I was now gazing out of.

Had the girl's bed been here, under the window? Had the girl awakened at the sound of the door opening?

If the Weaver family had been less connected, if the county attorney had filed charges against Jane Weaver and the case had gone to trial, there would have been testimony, a record, a judgment from the jury that controlled the version of the events we believed and afforded us an official, if not perfectly definitive, answer to the question: Was Elizabeth's death a tragic accident or murder?

The realtor cleared her throat and asked if I wanted to see the basement.

"Sure," I said.

The basement was unfinished, with cinder block walls and a cement floor. The realtor and I walked past a wall of shelves, stacked with army-green duffels containing sleeping bags that the Lutheran kids must have used when they went on church retreats. A piece of plywood was nailed next to the shelves. On the plywood, someone had painted BEWARE OF THE BOOGEYMAN.

Startled, I looked at the realtor. She was gazing off into the distance with a pleasant expression, as if she were completely unaware of the strange words on the plywood, as if they weren't even there.

The words were green. Tails of paint trailed down from the letters.

Who had written them?

Maybe one of the Weaver kids, decades earlier, had painted them as part of a game they were playing. Or maybe one of the Lutheran kids had done it when he was down in the basement, putting the sleeping bags away, a little uneasy because he knew what had happened in the house years ago, and how could you not be anxious in this basement, floors below the place where a girl had died at her mother's hands?

In the way that I needed the rape to fit the familiar cautionary tale, authors of the different versions of the Weaver murder needed Elizabeth's death to fill some particular purpose.

What kind of moral do you want Elizabeth Weaver's death to support? If you see the story as representative of how rich people receive favorable treatment, you'd take the hallucination as a cover-up for a deliberate murder (after all, the cause of the girl's death was strangulation, not smothering, a factual inconsistency). The county attorney's failure to file charges would be his calculated attempt to maintain favor with a well-connected family (and, by extension, with all the well-connected families who were the Weavers' friends).

Or is the Weaver murder a story of the horror of mental illness, of a mother so deep in her delusion that she couldn't distinguish smothering from strangling? Is it a story of one family's specific tragedy?

I wonder how many Lincoln girls, in the days after the murder made the paper, glanced—as I did, warily and momentarily—at their mothers, and told themselves, that's not a story that has anything to do with my life. My mother's not like that, she'd never hurt me. And then created their own comforting versions of what happened.

Chapter 20 :: **Omaha, 1985**

While my parents and I sat in M's Pub on Monday, July 22, 1985, the jury that heard the testimony in *State of Nebraska v. Joe N. Griffin* began their deliberations. They discussed the case for forty-five minutes that afternoon, broke for the weekend, and then resumed their discussion on Monday morning. They returned their verdict at 12:28 p.m. on Monday. All told, they discussed the evidence for slightly more than four hours.

When Ivory calls, I'm in the living room of the apartment I share with Abby. Abby's at her job at the pharmacy on the west side of town. I've just gone into the kitchen to dump the ashtray in the garbage and am setting it back on the table. Missy stands next to me, wagging her tail. Lloyd Cole's

Easy Pieces spins on the stereo. The window that looks out on Harney Street is open a few inches and a warm breeze tangles the curtains.

The phone rings.

I suspect the call is from Ivory, and my heart begins to beat a little too hard, even though I've been waiting all weekend to hear, waiting months, in fact, for this moment. I hope it's Ivory with news. With good news. If it's bad news, I don't want to know, not yet. In the seconds between the first and second ring of the phone, I'm suspended in a time of not-knowing, a time when I'm holding on to the belief that Diane and Tara and I were utterly convincing, that the jury found Griffin guilty, that the whole episode will shortly be closed off, finished like a story with the deserved outcome, the protagonists rewarded, the offender punished.

At the same time, I feel uneasy: perhaps the verdict was reached so quickly because the jury didn't believe us. Didn't believe us at all.

I lift the receiver. I say hello.

It *is* Ivory. He says, "We did it," and tells me that the jury found Griffin guilty on all three counts of first-degree forcible sexual assault and the three counts of using a knife to commit a felony.

I sit down in the rocking chair. Across from me, the window that looks out over Harney Street shows the sky, cloudy and pale gray, above the surrounding landscape. Holding the phone against my ear, I am conscious that my perception of the sky has shifted. The grayness has become softer. Relief has as much power as many months of dread to alter the way one sees the natural world.

I must have thanked Ivory; he probably told me the date when the sentencing was scheduled, but what I remember most clearly is looking out the window at the sky.

•

Joe N. Griffin's sentencing was scheduled for October 1985. That fall, I continued working at my two part-time jobs, as a reservationist at Ramada in the afternoons and evenings, and on Friday mornings and Sunday afternoons at the library in the Methodist/Children's Hospital on 72nd and Dodge. On Fridays, I worked with another library clerk, and plenty of people came through—doctors, nurses, pharmacy assistants, who leafed through the *Physician's Desk Reference* or sat at one of the tables and filled out medical reports. Sundays were different; I was the only staff person there, and hardly anyone came in over the course of my four-hour shift.

The silence made me nervous. Anyone could enter the library, any person making his way into the building and onto the elevator, up to the sixth floor, and then through the heavy double doors to the library, which was at the end of a quiet hallway.

So Jim came to work with me on Sundays. We'd stop for lunch beforehand; then he'd read his gross anatomy text in one of the library carrels, getting up occasionally to go to the hallway for a drink of water. I sat behind the circulation desk and looked through medical books. I studied pictures of disgusting fungal infections that caused something that looked like hair to grow on people's tongues. I saw a photo of a man whose hernia had grown so extreme that he carted the protrusion in front of him in a wheelbarrow.

Also that fall, the Chicago Bears began what would become their storied championship season. Jim's TV was in the bedroom of his condo, and he, Missy, and I sat on the bed, watching the cocky quarterback McMahon, the stocky Fridge—who sportscasters had started calling a folk hero—and running back Walter Payton, who bulldozed his way through defensive linemen and knocked players in the face when they tried to tackle him. Jim loved the Bears; he laughed at their antics and trick plays and gleefully pounded the mattress when they scored a touchdown.

I applied to graduate school, the MA program in English at the University of Nebraska, back home in Lincoln. Abby began dating one of her classmates, a guy who'd been a Sig Ep with Jim and was a couple of years younger than us. She and I took up jogging. We both had Walkmans, so we listened to REM tapes while we ran. The Walkmans were heavy, slightly larger than a mass-market paperback, and our hands sweated against the vinyl cases. Our route took us down Saddle Creek Road toward the strip mall where Target and Hinky Dinky were located, and then up a steep stretch that led to a church. We called that part of the run the Mother Hill, and when we got up the incline we always had to stop, gasping for breath, our hands on our knees.

Daylight Savings ended. The days cooled. By the time Joe Griffin was sentenced, it had been almost a year since he'd attacked Diane as she was walking home from Schaffer's, the grocery store around the corner from the apartment where Abby and I used to live; ten months from the time he'd attacked Tara; eight months since he'd attacked me.

•

The sentencing was scheduled for the afternoon of Wednesday, October 16, 1985, in the same courtroom where the trial had been held. I went to the hearing alone and sat near the spot my parents had occupied during the trial itself. Neither Diane nor Tara were there. I would never know why. Joe Griffin, dressed again in his orange jumpsuit, sat facing the judge's bench. I had a notion of what might happen: The judge would walk in, announce the number of years of the sentence, and leave. And then Joe N. Griffin would be led past me; he might look over; I might make eye contact and give him a tiny, cold smile that said *Got you*; or I might look determinedly away, ignoring him as if he didn't exist.

The judge entered the courtroom. We rose, then sat. I held my hands folded in my lap. I was wearing one of my fall-weight Kathryn Conover dresses, striped navy and gray with navy velvet trim on the collar. My purse rested on the floor at my feet.

The judge seated himself. He looked out over his bench. Griffin stood. The judge announced the sentence: eight to ten years in prison for each of the three sexual assault charges. Five to eight years in prison for each of the three counts of using a knife to commit a felony. The six prison terms were to be served consecutively. Why the range of numbers? I wondered. I'd learn the answer to this question years later in law school; a sentence with a range of time to be served, rather than a specific number of years, was called an indeterminate sentence, and the minimum and maximum dates would be used by Department of Corrections attorneys in calculating dates for parole, early release, and mandatory release. Decades later an investigation would reveal that by ignoring a Nebraska Supreme Court ruling on the proper formula for these calculations, the DOC attorneys had allowed prisoners to be released too early.

Sitting in the courtroom, I began doing the math—a maximum of ten years times three, plus eight years times three, was fifty-four years, but the minimum was twenty-four plus fifteen.

Then I realized the judge was still speaking.

"Having gone through that trial, having heard that evidence, I am convinced that the jury returned the correct verdict," Judge Gitnick said. His voice was even and measured, though I heard—or thought I heard—an undercurrent of anger. "What you did to those young women was despicable."

I found myself sitting up straighter in surprise. The judge was allowed to do that, to verbally reprimand the rapist? This public censure, this scolding, was what I wanted all along. The judge was saying, *I believed those girls who testified.* Gitnick was telling Griffin that he was a scumbag. *Thank you,* I wanted to say. *Thank you.*

"What troubles me," Judge Gitnick went on, "is that you seem to feel that you are not guilty. I honestly don't know how you rationalize that." He suggested that perhaps the long sentence in prison would give Joe N. Griffin an opportunity to reflect and come to some understanding of his culpability.

Because Griffin never admitted his guilt, his motives remained unknown. Rape isn't about sex; it's about power and anger, and presumably Griffin felt a thrill of satisfaction when he spotted a potential victim, got close enough to flash the knife in front of her face, and made his threats. But what exactly had happened in his past to turn him into a man who walked the streets around the med center looking for small women he could easily overpower? Was he the grown version of the mean boys on the playground at Elliott, who had learned by second grade that violence permitted them to achieve a certain standing in the world? How did Joe N. Griffin explain his own behavior to himself?

Joe N. Griffin stared straight ahead. Judge Gitnick finished speaking, tapped his gavel, and left. I was grateful for the judge's reprimand; I felt like I'd gotten almost everything I wanted, except the answers to questions I'd never be able to ask Griffin: *What was your motivation? Why did you do it? Why me?*

I watched a deputy lead Griffin out of the courtroom. He didn't look over to where I was sitting. Maybe he hadn't even noticed I was there.

•

The following afternoon, I sat at the desk in my bedroom on Harney Street, facing the window that looked out on the parking lot. The sun shone in over my typewriter and cast a square of light on the hardwood floor. Missy lay on the bed. I was reading the article published in the Omaha *World Herald* about the sentencing. "Gitnick ordered that the six prison terms be served one after the other."Officials estimated Griffin would have to serve 26 years in prison before he can be considered for parole."

Finally, someone had spelled out the math, had given a number I could hold in my head. Twenty-six years. I was twenty-three years old. In twenty-six years, I'd be forty-nine. Forty-nine! It seemed like an unimaginably long time away. A comforting unimaginably long time away. By the time I was forty-nine, I thought, I'd be living somewhere other than Omaha. I'd be married; I'd have a different last name. I would have disappeared into the rest of my life, and there would be no way Joe N. Griffin could find me when he got out.

I figured he'd want revenge after all those years in prison. Isn't that what always happened in the movies—the criminal gets out of jail and goes after the person he believes is responsible for putting him there?

But I didn't have to think about that right now. Even if I wasn't married, even if I happened to still be in Nebraska, twenty-six years was decades away. I would be safe for a long time. I could put Joe N. Griffin out of my mind. Surely Diane and Tara had read the paper or seen the news. Surely we were sharing the same sense of relief. But—likely out of sharing the same need to move on—we would never compare notes. I would never see either of them again.

I cut out the article, filed it in the drawer of the desk, and stuffed the rest of the paper in the trash can. The smell of newsprint reminded me of Sunday mornings years earlier, sitting on the couch next to my father with the paper and hearing the story of how the Nebraska state capitol was one of the Seven Wonders of the World.

Chapter 21 :: **Lincoln, 1992**

On Wednesday, December 2, 1992, the sky was spitting snow. Exhaustion and anxiety permeated the campus: the end of the semester was a week away with finals looming, papers to write, too much to do. And the weather had added its own troubles, freezing car batteries and leaving dangerous slick patches on steps and giving everyone colds. Students trudged between buildings, bundled in parkas and scarves. I taught my two composition classes in the morning, glancing now and then through the window to see if the weather was holding or getting worse. This time of year, it could go either way.

In the gloomy afternoon, Yogi and I took our usual constitutional along 27th Street toward the Children's Zoo. Yogi loved the cold. He lifted his nose, sniffing deeply, while the wind flattened his fur against his skull. We crunched over patches of snow on the sidewalk. I felt my fingers numbing inside my gloves.

The flyers with Candice Harms's picture that had been taped to light poles were now faded beyond recognition or had been torn away. Still, we hadn't forgotten her. There were plans to put up additional billboards after the first of the year.

On Wednesday, December 2, the mystery of Candice Harms remained unsolved. But that day, authorities arrested Scott Barney and Roger Bjorklund after an attempted robbery of the Goodyear Federal Credit Union at 5700 Seward Street, out in Havelock, a neighborhood on the north side of town. The men were taken into custody and charged with the Goodyear robbery, as well as two others: Rex's TV on September 16 and a later robbery of Goodyear Credit Union on September 30, the two crimes that had bookended Candice Harms's disappearance.

At this point, police had no suspects in the Harms case other than Todd Sears, who had been interviewed again and again. Authorities had no idea that the two robbery suspects they'd just taken into custody were the ones responsible for Candice's disappearance until four days later.

On Sunday, December 6, Kirk Naylor—Scott Barney's attorney, considered one of the best defense lawyers in town—contacted the police and said his client wanted to talk about the missing girl. Barney had information about her. He would take them to her body.

Barney directed police to that field five miles southeast of Lincoln at 134th and Yankee Hill Road, where a single cottonwood tree stretched its bare branches above the frozen ground. In his orange jumpsuit, he stepped out of the backseat of the police car, pointed to the tree, and got back in the vehicle. The officers trudged across the snowy field. A bitter wind pressed into their faces. About ten feet from the cottonwood, Lincoln police detective sergeant Noah Van Butsel saw part of a bone protruding from the snow.

Investigators found a body buried from the mid-chest up. The lower part of the body, which had been exposed to the elements, had mostly skeletonized—only bones remained. As the snow melted and the dirt was moved away, a watch became visible, strapped to the body's left wrist. The watch was still running, ticking off seconds and minutes, though it read an hour ahead—an hour into the future—still set for Daylight Savings Time, which hadn't ended until weeks after Candice Harms had disappeared on September 22.

What mixed emotions the officers must have had as they uncovered more bones beneath the cottonwood tree, the bitterness of having to break this news outweighing any relief in resolution.

Candice Harms's mother Pat was sweeping snow off the porch when Sheriff Tom Casady drove up to tell her what they'd found.

•

What moved Barney to confess? After all, authorities had no idea he and Bjorklund were connected to the crime. Candice's body had remained undiscovered all these months, the guns below the frozen surface of Pawnee Lake, the burned clothing and blanket now buried under snow. Barney and Bjorklund had used Lincoln itself to cover their tracks—all those empty spaces on the edges of the town, the distances between where they abandoned the Corsica on the far north side, the rape and the burned clothing miles east of there, the girl murdered and buried in a field on the southern outskirts of the city. Everything done in the middle of the night when there was no one around to see; all the evidence spread out so that it would be difficult, perhaps impossible, to locate, let alone put together. If Barney hadn't spoken up, the Candice Harms case might have remained unsolved for years, though her body would likely have been discovered when the field where she was buried was tilled for spring planting.

There's a conventional narrative in which the criminal, consumed by guilt, comes clean to assuage his conscience, thereby giving some answers, some closure, to the suffering victims of his crime. Moved by altruism, the criminal would like you to believe. Wanting to make things right. Showing he's reformed and regretful.

Some people believe these narratives. Many people don't.

Perhaps Barney imagined that the cops were closing in on him and Bjorklund even though they weren't. He might have feared that Bjorklund would confess and implicate Barney himself as the primary perpetrator. By speaking up first, Barney was able to control the narrative and use his knowledge—where the body was buried, where the guns had been thrown—to arrange a plea bargain. Barney told the story in a way that pinned the bulk of the blame on Bjorklund: Bjorklund was the one who'd actually abducted the girl, the one who shot her twice when she lay face down in the field and then shot her again when he returned for a blanket the men had left behind. The electric chair hadn't been used since the Starkweather execution in 1959, and Barney's agreement to plead guilty to first-degree murder as long as prosecutors didn't pursue the death penalty guaranteed that he'd be spared Charlie Starkweather's fate.

•

On Monday morning, December 7, 1992, authorities announced that Roger Bjorklund and Scott Barney were suspects in the Candice Harms case. At that point, no charges had been filed, and Lancaster County Attorney Gary Lacey said, "I am not prepared to tell you that they will be charged. We should know in a week." The attorneys working the case would need this time to finalize the plea agreement with Scott Barney, to parse the evidence they had to determine the precise crimes they could prove.

Monday marked the beginning of the last week of the fall 1992 semester. In the 8:30 a.m. composition class, students were giving oral reports on current issues. Troy announced that he'd planned to talk about campus parking—a perennial topic of concern and outrage among the students—but that he'd changed his mind because something more important had occurred: Candice Harms had been found.

The class discussed what they knew from newspaper reports and new rumors circulating around campus. Troy shared one of these rumors, that the two suspects had sat in a parking lot near the university, waiting for night class to be over. "Where did you hear that?" I asked.

"A girl in my dorm."

I wanted to push—ask the girl's name, how she'd come across this information—but I remembered their resistance during the discussion about urban legends, the spring break romance that turned horribly wrong. The facts of what had happened the evening Candice Harms disappeared—or the official version, at least—would come out soon enough, and this bit of information would turn out to be true.

Listening to the students talk, I thought back to the first day of class in August. A hot morning, the way August mornings in Lincoln tend to be. As I'd walked down the wide hallway on the first floor of Andrews Hall, I saw that the classroom door was open, but the room itself was still dark.

Since it was nearly 8:30, I'd been surprised: I figured at least one person would've arrived by then, gone inside, and turned on the overhead lights.

I stepped into the classroom, expecting to find it empty. Instead, all the students were there, seated around the table, absolutely silent, hands folded, waiting.

They were all first-year students. This class was their very first college course. They were seventeen or eighteen years old; some were from the big cities of Lincoln and Omaha, but others had come from towns out west with populations smaller than the dorms they now lived in. Every one of them had been too shy and polite to disturb anything in the room. They'd all known that flicking the light switch would have come across to the others as pushy.

Candice Harms might have been on campus herself then, in a different classroom, waiting for a professor to step to the front of the room and hand around a syllabus. She'd been among us, and then she'd disappeared. The mystery of what had happened to her permeated the semester. Now we had an answer to the mystery, and the semester was coming to a close, with more than the usual mixture of relief and regret. That morning in December, I looked at the students' faces, which had altered in barely perceptible ways: some looked a little thinner or heavier, some pale without their summer tans. I thought how much they'd changed in the few months I'd known them. They'd turn in their final projects at the end of class and go off into the rest of their lives. Most of them I'd never see again.

•

Walking Yogi along the snow-crusted bike path on the afternoon of December 7, I thought about the balmy night three months earlier when Candice Harms disappeared. I remembered the weather. I remembered my unease. If what Troy had said that morning were true, that the killers had waited in a university parking lot for night classes to end, then perhaps I owed a debt to whatever prescience made me bring Yogi along.

Which lot had they been in? Was it the one Yogi and I crossed? How many of us on campus came closer than we realized to encountering Barney and Bjorklund? How many other girls in the city were possibly spared that night by the accidental presence of others—drunk frat brothers suddenly stumbling out of an alley, a bicyclist turning a corner, cruising teenagers deciding, on a whim, to take the long route home that led them past a girl walking alone and oblivious?

And later, once the murderers' presence on campus that night was confirmed, how many of us would experience something akin to survivor's guilt, as Abby did after my rape, going so far as to put herself at risk?

I'd never know which lot the killers sat in. Still, I couldn't stop thinking about it as Yogi and I walked the path behind the Children's Zoo, both of us squinting against driving snow. I understood that we are all granted a finite amount of good luck. I wondered how much of my own portion remained.

Chapter 22 :: **Lincoln, 1981 and 1991**

When did the downtown Hovland Swanson's store close? I can't remember; I can't recall the last time I stepped foot in the store, though I know it was years after I'd taken the White Gloves and Party Manners class. I remember riding the elevator up to the juniors' department, looking at the clothes that were priced a ways beyond my budget, staying around long enough to suggest I wasn't leaving because I couldn't afford anything; rather, I was leaving because I didn't find anything I wanted.

But when was that, exactly? I must've gone into Hovland's in college. In the end, it wasn't a store deeply imprinted in my memory, though I can still call up the shoe department, the name of the clerk there who was my mother's friend, the fragrance of perfumed scarves on the first floor.

I do remember the closing of Gold's, in 1981. My mother had worked at Gold's before she was married. She'd bought her wedding dress there, a knee-length cocktail dress made of beige raw silk with a narrow skirt and sleeves that hit an inch above the elbows. The dress cost $32.95, less her fifteen-percent employee discount. She'd known Mr. Gold—"a true gentleman," she said—who walked through the store every morning, greeting the clerks by name. After the greetings, there was an official moment of silence before the store opened, which established a kind of gravity, a kind of seriousness, to the endeavor of commerce.

Gold's intent was to stock everything a shopper could possibly want, so the store had—in addition to clothing, furniture, shoes, toys, books, and housewares—hosiery and sundries on the first floor, a whole section of shampoos and foot powders, hairbrushes, and deodorants. My mother bought me my first pair of pantyhose in Gold's. Abby and I went to Gold's for our tins of henna when we were in high school. We bought ourselves rings in the jewelry department, the bands made of delicate chains set with tiny chips of semi-precious stones, a sapphire for me and an emerald for Abby. Abby and I liked, but didn't love, Gold's. It wasn't the first store we went to when shopping for new clothes. Actually, Gold's wasn't really Gold's anymore; the store had been sold to Brandeis, a department store headquartered in Omaha, in 1964. In the Brandeis corporation, the store was known as "Brandeis, Gold's Division." Nonetheless, my mother persisted, as did many other Lincolnites, in referring to the store as Gold's, even on the pay-to-the-order line of her checks, which the Brandeis clerks glanced at and filed, without comment, in the drawers of their cash registers. You could tell yourself that even though things appeared to change, they really hadn't.

And then, in 1980, Brandeis decided to liquidate the store.

At first, I found the liquidation exciting: the marked-down prices, the way the merchandise got jumbled together so that you could occasionally turn up unexpected treasures—the brown pumps that I found in the linens area next to a stack of sheets, for instance. But as the liquidation continued, as more goods were sold off, as the character of the shoppers changed—they'd become predatory and careless, pawing through tables of goods, knocking items on the floor and leaving them there—the store became less familiar, a strange place with dark pockets where departments had been emptied out, the lights turned off. Bare racks, bits of tissue and gum wrappers dropped on the floor and not picked up, fingerprint smears on the glass cases in the jewelry department, no jewelry inside. Fewer and fewer clerks, longer lines at the cash registers, merchandise stuffed carelessly into bags.

The store closed officially in the late winter of 1981. The Gold's building became just an enormous empty structure in the middle of downtown, unused and waiting to be given some sort of purpose.

Shoppers who favored Gold's mourned its passing. Driving on 10th Street, my mother would say, "It's too bad it's gone," and make the same little regretful noise she did when we passed by the lot where Herpolsheimer's—Lincoln's first department store—once stood, a Victorian fabrication with turrets and fretwork that I knew only from photographs. In fact, my mother herself had never been in Herpolsheimer's, as the store had closed in 1931, before she was born, but we owned some items that had been purchased there, a china teapot, for instance, that had been a wedding gift to her parents—and so the ghostly presence of that store lived on for her.

But even after Gold's was closed, Miller and Paine was still in business. Miller's was my favorite place to shop, and I believed that the store would be there forever.

•

I was working at Miller's in 1988 at the store in the Gateway Shopping Center, which had sprung up on the east side of town in the 1960s. Newcomers to Lincoln referred to Gateway as The Mall, but we natives called it simply Gateway. My department, named The Eclectic Company, stocked contemporary home décor items. It was located next to the Tearoom where I'd worked in high school.

One day in June, I felt a definite shift in the atmosphere, the sort of tension you sense in the air before a thunderstorm hits. The store managers scurried around; department heads were called to the conference room behind Customer Service. I stood next to the cash register and exchanged puzzled glances with my friend Clinton, who worked in the bakery. Something was going on, but what could it be?

Shortly the news came out that a national department store chain was buying Miller and Paine.

The true shock—that Miller's would cease to exist as Miller's—was mitigated by assurances that nothing would change, and, for a time, nothing did. The name on the outside of the Miller and Paine buildings became Dillard's, but inside it was the same. At the downtown store, once you pushed through the revolving doors, the interior still breathed Miller's: the same distinctive smell, the various departments exactly where they'd always been, the familiar merchandise (though the price tags were different, cream-colored instead of the grayish shade Miller's had used), the same clerks standing behind the counters—Rose wiping down the glass cases in the candy department, Betty delivering food in the basement cafeteria, the woman whose name I never knew but who had been at Miller's forever still sitting in her little nook on the first floor and pushing buttons on the machine that ticked out Blue Stamps.

Three years passed before the Dillard's people decided to liquidate the downtown location in 1991. Already many of the familiar stores were gone. Gold's had closed. Sears and JC Penney's had relocated to Gateway. Sandy's Bar had moved from the corner of 14th and O to 11th Street between O and P, a tidy space with fresh carpet, new chairs, and wall writing expressly forbidden; it was not the Sandy's I remembered. Like department stores in downtowns all over the country, the downtown Dillard's wasn't doing enough business to justify keeping it open. In the winter and spring of 1991, merchandise was marked down and sold. Clerks consolidated the remaining goods in a haphazard fashion, so you'd find yourself browsing through a collection of women's blouses, training bras, and men's trousers all bunched together on a single rack where the records used to be.

On one of the last days the store was open, I rode the escalator all the way to the top floor and then made my way back down, stopping on each floor and walking through the almost-empty departments.

The Tearoom, on the fifth floor, had been closed for months. The fabric department was dark. Schoolhouse lights still hung from the ceiling; the counters—where pattern books had laid open, tempting women to stop for just a moment and browse through the pages—were bare. How many hours of my life, I wondered, had I spent in that department, waiting while my mother went through patterns. I remembered the tilt of her head when she studied something she liked, the way she'd lick her right index finger before she turned the page.

On the third floor, the pre-teen department—where I'd purchased my first bra, some spectacularly small size, like a 30AAA, back in sixth grade—

was vacant; the business office was shuttered. No music played over the speakers. The only sound came from the escalators, endlessly moving, the lurch between the first and second floors keeping faithful time.

I walked past the space where the bridal department had been on the second floor. I remembered the day I'd tried on a wedding dress when I was in ninth grade. I remembered Cathy, the clerk who'd suggested it. I remembered the boy from Shipping and Receiving who'd walked through with his cart. The past and the present seemed to exist simultaneously, inside this building; effortlessly, I could see the empty departments filled, see my younger self browsing through racks, pausing, adopting the very mannerisms of my mother as she looked at patterns, with head tilted, eyes narrowing in evaluation.

Now, in the spring of 1991, empty plastic hangers filled the racks in the bridal department. They tapped together like wind chimes when you brushed against them. Signs taped to the counters said *Fixtures for sale*. Disassembled mannequins lay in corners, wigless, the seams on their wrists visible, the red paint on their fingernails scratched and chipping.

The cots were gone from the Ladies' Lounge. They'd been removed a couple of years earlier because homeless people were going there to sleep.

I rode the escalator down from the second floor. I crossed the polished marble floors of the main level, pushed through the revolving doors into the foyer, where the little display windows set into the wall were empty of merchandise, and stepped outside. I could feel a knot of emotion tightening in my throat, so I took a deep breath and started walking south on 13th Street. This year—1991—I'd turn thirty, and I felt, in some ways, as if I'd become a much older person, someone looking back from a long distance at her youth and mourning all the places that were gone.

Chapter 23 :: **Lincoln, 1993–1994**

The trial of the *State of Nebraska v. Roger Bjorklund* began on Monday, October 25, 1993, a little over a year after Candice Harms had disappeared. Because pre-trial publicity precluded the possibility of an impartial local jury, jurors had been chosen in Sidney—350 miles away in western Nebraska—and brought to Lincoln to hear the case.

Lancaster County Attorney Gary Lacey laid out the timeline of the two men's grisly plan. The search for a victim, the waiting in the university parking lot for night class to get out. The girl abducted by Bjorklund. Her vehicle abandoned on Bluff Road. Candice taken to 86th and Havelock Avenue. Raped by both men. Driven to Yankee Hill Road and murdered.

Pat Harms, Candice's mother, described the clothing Candice had been wearing the night she disappeared. An employee from Maurice's clothing store testified that a green BUM jacket submitted as evidence "is from the same manufacturer's lot as the one Harms put on layaway and eventually purchased at the store." That was the jacket she was wearing the night she disappeared.

Detectives took the stand and described crossing the field at 134th and Yankee Hill Road, seeing bones protruding from snow, and finding the girl's body.

A police investigator told of searching the banks of Stevens Creek in the cold afternoon and evening of December 6, 1992. The following afternoon, he located the ash pile of burned clothing.

The landlord who owned the house rented by Roger Bjorklund testified he'd gone to the house to repair a washer and found a .38-caliber shell under the machine.

On Thursday, November 4, coroner's physician Matthias Okoye told jurors that autopsy results convinced him that Candice Harms had been sexually tortured before her death. The *Journal* noted that "[t]he most chilling photos and testimony came when Okoye showed jurors photos of Harms's chest area—where some skin remained intact—and told them that one of her nipples had been removed." Okoye also noted numerous small cuts found around her breast and arm that appeared to have been inflicted with a sharp instrument similar to a surgical knife.

One of Bjorklund's attorneys, the deputy public defender Richard Goos, objected and questioned whether the cuts could have been inflicted by underbrush and whether the nipple could have been "removed by animals."

Okoye repeated that, in his professional opinion, the injuries were consistent with torture.

Jurors heard tapes of Bjorklund arguing with a police detective regarding certain aspects of his case. The first taped statement had been made on December 6, 1992, the day after Barney had come forward with information about Harms. The Lincoln *Journal* related what the statement revealed: Describing the events that took place the night the girl disappeared, Bjorklund told Detective Sergeant Greg Sorensen that "I have my own religious theories about why we [Bjorklund and Barney] were both out of control and I was hoping we would get caught 'cuz [sic] I was tired of living my life that way." Bjorklund also told Sorensen that it was Barney's idea to "silence Harms completely. . . . And me being the dumb follower that I was went along with it."

Bjorklund claimed Barney had shot Candice twice in the head as she lay face down in the field. When Bjorklund returned to retrieve the blanket the men had left behind, he realized she was still breathing. He decided that he "couldn't let her suffer," so he shot her five times.

The second taped conversation took place on May 25, 1993. At Bjorklund's request, he'd been taken to the police station to talk to Sorensen and Detective Sergeant Sandra Myers. In this conversation, Bjorklund said Barney had lied to minimize his (Barney's) involvement. Bjorklund denied physically torturing Harms. He also claimed he hadn't seen Barney torturing her. Bjorklund was upset that certain newspaper articles had mentioned him as the only one to shoot Harms when he felt that Barney was equally guilty.

The trial lasted three weeks and ended on Monday, November 15. Neither Barney nor Bjorklund had taken the stand. In their closing statements, the prosecution said that Bjorklund's taped conversations clearly proved his guilt. The defense argued that these statements weren't voluntary, that police had induced Bjorklund to confess by providing soda pop, cigarettes, and possibly pizza. Moreover, the defense argued, there was a question of which man had fired the shots that actually killed Candice Harms. Chief Deputy Public Defender Scott Helvie said there was evidence that shots fired by Barney killed Harms. In short, the prosecution had failed to prove Bjorklund's guilt "beyond a reasonable doubt."

The jury of eight women and four men began their deliberations at 1:53 p.m. that afternoon.

•

After discussing the case for a little more than thirteen hours, the jury returned their verdict on the morning of Wednesday, November 14, 1993. They found Bjorklund guilty of first-degree murder and use of a weapon to commit a felony in the abduction, rape, and murder of Candice Harms.

According to newspaper reports, when the verdict was read, Bjorklund turned to look at his wife, Shannon, who sat in the third row of the courtroom, weeping.

Prosecutors intended to pursue the death penalty against Bjorklund at the sentencing hearing, which was scheduled to begin on January 24, 1994. Judge Donald Endacott would determine the sentence.

The Harms family spoke to reporters after the verdict. The longer the jury deliberated, the more they'd worried about the decision, but they were relieved to hear the outcome. Candice's father Stan thought that both Bjorklund and Barney deserved the death penalty, but Barney, of course, had made the deal to save himself from that fate. Stan Harms said that he saw "no redeeming value in Bjorklund, who appears to have no remorse."

•

In January, Lancaster County District Court Judge Donald Endacott sentenced Bjorklund to death. Scott Barney, meanwhile, had begun serving his sentence of life in prison in June 1994. He is currently incarcerated in the Tecumseh State Correctional Facility, located two miles north of Tecumseh, Nebraska, a small town of approximately 1,700 in the southeast corner of the state.

•

On death row at the Nebraska State Penitentiary, Roger Bjorklund sent the following pen-pal request to the Canadian Coalition against the Death Penalty's website, which offered "free webpages to Death Row Prisoners":

> I have been on death row since September 20, 1994. I am interested in a lot of different things. First and foremost would be sports. I have always been involved in sports in one way or another. I like to watch football, my favorite teams in the NFL are St. Louis and the NY Jets, of course I am a Nebraska Cornhusker fan. I also enjoy auto racing of all types, NBA Basketball, baseball, and boxing. I enjoy reading, writing and music, mostly Country and Rock. I am 32 years old and was born March 16th. I was in the computer profession for many years and I owned my own computer store. I lived all over the U.S. mostly in Nevada. I was adopted when I was 6 days old and was raised on a ranch in Nebraska. I look forward to hearing from a pen-pal. Please take really good care of yourselves and be safe. Sincerely—

Chapter 24 :: Connections and Disconnections

The novelist and memoirist Robert Goolrick says that memoirs are written records of "the stories we tell ourselves about our lives." I had, indeed, told myself a story about Lincoln, this city in the middle of the country that was the site of one of the Seven Wonders of the World. What I found most comforting about living in Lincoln was the fact that I understood the place—and the people—on a level that went below the surface. The town was filled with subtext. I could see a girl walking up Van Dorn Street at 4 o'clock on a fall afternoon, take in the details of her appearance—the long hair, leggings, backpack slung over one shoulder (but not both), the way she walked slowly, staring at the ground—and I'd know she was walking home from Southeast, that she'd stayed after school for some reason (maybe having a fight with her boyfriend, a fight that didn't go well, given her pensive expression). She was a pretty-enough girl. She was wearing the right sort of clothes; often I could make an educated guess as to where she'd bought them, and a shirt from Hovland's told me something different about her than a shirt from Miller and Paine. She carried her backpack in the self-conscious fashion the kids had recently adopted (putting both straps over your shoulders was a look for geeks). I'd see this girl, and I understood her situation, because I'd been in that situation myself before. In her, I saw a younger version of myself.

Nearly everything I saw in Lincoln could pull me back into the comforting past. Like two girls walking together along 33rd Street, one of them with a laundry bag slung over her shoulder, the other carrying a cooler. They both wore black shorts and light-colored t-shirts, and bumped companionably against each other as they made their way down the sidewalk. Abby and I had walked on that same street years and years ago, dressed alike, talking and laughing, and every time I saw two girls walking together, I'd think: best friends.

I knew the story behind the various buildings, like the Weaver house and places that had once been grocery stores. Walking Yogi, I'd see a Von Busch refuse truck, and the name Von Busch called to mind Bob Von Busch, who'd been friends with Charlie Starkweather. I could contemplate the details of the town, see connections, and construct a story that made all kinds of sense. This behavior was, perhaps, a bit like that of the Puritans in New England, who examined every daily occurrence for evidence of God's favor. The bountiful harvest, the discovery of wild blueberries, the easeful fitting of fabric squares in the construction of a quilt: how rich their ordinary and often stressful lives must have seemed, when everything connected in some way to a larger picture. And the Puritans were masterful at rationalization, as well. Their constant assessment of daily events was both humble, done in the spirit of interpreting divine will, and prideful, demonstrating a relentless focus on themselves. You might call it a form of cognitive dissonance. Even tragedy—a barn burned down by the Indians, the death of a child—could be interpreted as the working of God in your life: He was testing you, and your continued belief in His mercy demonstrated your devotion. You found details that supported the story you wanted to believe, that you were chosen. Chosen, special, one of the elect. Lives gleamed with meaning.

•

Of course I told myself the story of Lincoln in a way that preserved an overarching sense of safety and predictability. Even if some things had to be rationalized for the sake of that narrative. After Barney and Bjorklund were captured, after the details of their confession were revealed in the newspaper, I knew without doubt that even the worst people were capable of understanding how the town worked.

•

What really happened the night Candice Harms was murdered? Barney's version establishes Bjorklund as the primary perpetrator, the one who'd actually abducted Harms and the one responsible for shooting her twice after he'd fallen on top of her in the field and again when he returned for the blanket.

Bjorklund, on the other hand, referred to himself as the dumb follower and claimed it was Barney's idea to "silence Harms completely." According to Bjorklund, Barney shot Harms twice after Bjorklund had fallen on top of her in the field off Yankee Hill Road. Bjorklund also mentioned, during his conversations with police, that the night of Candice Harms's abduction he was "hoping we'd get caught because I was tired of living my life that way."

The autopsy report showed that Harms had been shot twice with a .380-caliber semi-automatic pistol and five times with a .38 caliber revolver.

Someone considering these details might come to the conclusion that Barney bore more responsibility for the murder than he admitted. As a native Lincolnite, I fill in the subtext of the details, and am confident that Barney was, in fact, the mastermind of the crime.

Here's my take: Barney, as a Lincoln native, had developed a deep understanding of the town, which he used to pinpoint potential areas to cruise for victims (like the university parking lot) and, later, places to disperse evidence of the crime.

I believe that Barney did, in fact, shoot Harms. The .38 caliber revolver belonged to Bjorklund (the landlord found a shell from the gun under the washing machine in the house Bjorklund rented). Bjorklund admitted to shooting Harms five times, which the autopsy report corroborates. But there were also two shots from a different gun. Why would Bjorklund— who admitted he shot her five times—have used two different weapons? I'd wager Barney fired the first two shots with the .380-caliber semi-automatic pistol.

Before he confessed, Barney hired one of the best defense attorneys in town. Going to law school gives you a certain understanding of local attorneys' reputations, and I knew Kirk Naylor was good. He was the guy you'd want representing you if you were guilty.

What motivated Barney to confess? I take a clue from Bjorklund's testimony: the *hoping we'd get caught* suggests someone who might crack under pressure, or someone who feels guilty and might seek to assuage that guilt by confessing. Barney had to speak up first, arrange the plea agreement, frame the narrative to minimize his own guilt, and, in this way, save himself from the electric chair.

In the end, I can parse the details of the case, but the Candice Harms murder can't be fit into a comforting narrative structure. It's a true story far more terrible and shocking than the Welcome to the World of AIDS urban legend. On an otherwise unremarkable Tuesday night toward the end of September, she'd run across the sort of evil no one in Lincoln wanted to believe existed. And one of the most troubling aspects of the story was that the killer was a native, he was one of us.

In fact, Barney's roots went back as far as mine did. There was a connection, however tenuous, between his father and my own: my father and Arvid Barney—Scott Barney's father—attended high school together, the Lincoln Northeast class of 1952. In his senior picture in the Northeast Rockets yearbook, Arvid Barney wears a suit and tie, like all the other boys; he has short-cropped light hair, even features, a friendly smile. His courses focused on industrial arts, and he was a reserve member of the football team his freshman year as well as a varsity basketball player in tenth and twelfth grades. His senior year, Arvid served as president of the N Club, a group of athletes who'd earned letters in football, basketball, or track. "The main goal of this organization is to promote good sportsmanship and better athletics at Northeast," the yearbook says. There's a picture of Arvid talking to two other members of the N Club. They all have the clean-cut appearance of 1950s jocks; Arvid wears a plaid shirt and cuffed blue jeans, the other boys have on sweaters and dress pants.

In 1952, the Northeast Rockets basketball team won the district championship, defeating the Falls City Tigers. Arvid played a pivotal role in the first game of the "all-important state tourney" against North Platte, when "Northeast edged them out in an over-time with a free throw by Arvid Barney for a score of 48–47."

Even if you don't care about sports, you understand how a moment like that is one you'd spend the rest of your life looking back on: the moment you performed a dramatic public feat that established your pack as superior to another pack. And forty years later, in the cold months that ended 1992 and began 1993, Arvid Barney must have recollected his high school days as the best times of his life, a time when he walked down the halls of Northeast to friendly greetings from his classmates, knowing a smile bestowed upon a shy girl could make her blush with pleasure, knowing the younger kids looked up to him and saw him, as Arvid Barney saw himself, as a young man who'd have all kinds of wonderful things in his future.

At the end of his life, people in Lincoln would see the surname Barney, and no one would connect it with Arvid's high school accomplishment. They'd only know that Arvid Barney was the father of a killer.

Chapter 25 :: **What Is Gone**

Jim proposed in the summer of 1987, on a night at the beginning of June, the air not yet humid enough to make your clothes stick against your skin. I was unaware of his plans. I thought we were just going to the Old Market for a couple of drinks. On the ride downtown, we stopped at the light at 30th and Harney. A woman wearing satin tap pants and a satin camisole stood on the corner by a bus shelter. She approached the car on the driver's side. When she was close enough, she saw that Jim wasn't alone and backed away.

"Who was that?" I asked.

The light turned green.

"That was a prostitute," Jim said.

I'd never seen a prostitute before. I looked out the back window as we drove away. There she was, standing on the corner in her lingerie.

Jim and I drank gin and tonics at Spaghetti Works and smoked a couple of cigarettes. Jim said, "How about a carriage ride?" as if the thought had just occurred to him.

"Sure," I said.

We crossed the street and climbed into a carriage harnessed to a black horse with a shaggy mane. The carriage driver shook the reins and the pony moved forward, his hooves clopping along the brick streets. We passed M's Pub and turned onto Harney. Jim put his hand on my arm and pointed at a building on the opposite side of the street. "Look!"

"What?"

"Over there!"

Was there something going on? Or words written on the building I needed to read? I peered into the darkness. On the seat next to me, Jim was fumbling with his ankle.

"What's wrong?" I asked, a little impatiently.

He'd hidden the ring inside his sock and was trying to distract me while he extricated it. "Here," he said, handing me a small velvet box. "Will you marry me?"

My heart lurched in surprise. The pony's harness rattled musically when he tossed his head. A breeze twisted the fringe on the carriage's roof. "Yes," I said. I opened the box, and inside winked a marquis-cut diamond on a thin gold band.

•

If I'd stopped here, with the proposal, you'd assume the relationship had a happy ending.

We married in May 1988. The year of the engagement had been long distance and rocky. Jim had moved to California in August 1987 for the first year of his medical residency, and we'd started arguing about a lot of things, like my double-pierced ears—which he thought were kind of trashy—what sort of food to serve at our wedding reception, what I was going to do as far as changing my name (I'd decided not to change my name when I got married; he considered that unreasonable). The problems seemed, on the one hand, superficial, but at the same time they indicated deep divisions about aesthetics and expectations, conventions and control. In hindsight, we shouldn't have gotten married at all, but the invitations had been sent, the bridesmaids' dresses made, the food and liquor ordered: the sheer momentum of planning pushed us ahead with the ceremony.

The marriage lasted six weeks. The last time I saw him was the Fourth of July weekend in 1988. It used to take me hours to explain what had gone wrong—hours to detail every nuance of the deteriorating relationship, the screaming phone conversations, the anger that drove me to throw his toothbrush in the toilet—but now, all these years later, the old grudges no longer matter. I remember how calm he was the night I was attacked, the carefully planned engagement, his affection for Missy the pug. The story of the marriage can be told in a single sentence: *I was married for a little while in my twenties, but it didn't work out.*

•

Other people and pets connected with that time in my life are gone.

Missy died in the spring of 1992, a few weeks after I'd graduated from law school. She is buried in the backyard of the house on California Court, next to the garage, in a grave dug by my father and one of my law school classmates.

It's been years since I've talked to the woman I'm calling Abby, the girl who'd been my best friend since our junior year of high school. As we entered our thirties, our lives branched out in different directions. We lived in different cities. We came to have less and less in common. The last time I saw her, in 1999, she talked about how difficult it was to see everyone when she and her husband and children returned to Lincoln on vacations. They had to make choices. She said, "If you're not married and don't have kids, you're basically off our list."

I was unmarried and childless. I took myself off her list.

Ivory Griggs died on May 20, 1998, of lung cancer. I was leafing through the Nebraska Bar Association's magazine when I saw his name in the obituary column.

It was thirteen years after the trial. Although I'd thought of Ivory often, I'd never written to tell him so. And now it was too late.

People and their fucking problems, I thought.

•

I was forty years old, married to my second husband, and living in Washington, D.C., when I realized that the Nebraska state capitol was not one of the Seven Wonders of the World. Somehow I'd managed to sustain the notion that somewhere in the world, an official document existed that supported my belief, until the afternoon when I was standing in front of the Office of the Treasury, on Pennsylvania Avenue. I found myself thinking that it was a pretty interesting-looking building. In fact, Washington was full of magnificent statuary and art; Yogi and I liked walking to the Lincoln Mall, glancing up at the statue of Abraham Lincoln and then making our way through the Korean War Memorial. Looking at the Office of the Treasury, I thought it was odd that none of the buildings or statues in DC had made the Seven Wonders of the World list. This realization forced me to follow a trail of logic that I found myself resisting even as I finally understood the truth: if none of the DC buildings were on the list, the Nebraska state capitol probably wasn't one of the Seven Wonders of the World.

Had my father lied to me? We weren't a family given to teasing and exaggerating; I wondered if he'd misread something or I'd misremembered what he'd said. I kept reminding myself to ask him when I made one of my trips back to Lincoln, but I always forgot.

Yogi was fourteen years old in 2003 when he suffered a massive organ failure and had to be put to sleep. He'd lived in Lincoln, and Iowa City, and Washington, DC, where tourists would stop in the middle of the street to snap his picture and students at George Washington University dropped to their knees on the sidewalk to embrace him.

•

Scott Barney has grown old in the Tecumseh State Correctional Institution. In his prison photo, he wears a light gray sweatshirt with a t-shirt underneath. His goatee and short hair are speckled with gray. Wrinkles spread across his forehead and from the corners of his eyes. The eyes themselves glitter, and there's something off-putting about his expression: His lips curl in a little smirk, as if he thinks he's gotten away with something. And I suppose he has gotten away with something. He and his friend executed their fantasy of abducting and raping a woman. He understands what the act is like. He's not on death row. He's still alive, the only survivor of the three people involved in the incident of September 22, 1992.

In 1997, Bjorklund's wife Shannon divorced him. She changed her surname, as well as the surname of their two daughters, and moved away. The former Shannon Bjorklund intrigues me. I wonder how much she knew about what her husband was doing. Did she question where he was getting all the money he and Barney collected from their robberies? Did she awaken when he crawled into bed in the very early morning of September 23, 1992, and did she wonder where he'd been? How much, I wonder, is a woman capable of failing to see?

On July 1, 2001, Bjorklund was found ill in his cell. He attempted to communicate with the guards but was "incoherent." Taken to BryanLGH West, Bjorklund was pronounced dead at 8:19 a.m. A subsequent autopsy revealed that he was suffering from severe occlusive coronary artery disease, which caused an irregular heartbeat that led to his death.

His body was cremated at the state's expense, and the location of the ashes is undisclosed.

Chapter 26 :: Lincoln, Now

What of Joe N. Griffin, and what has happened to me?

After the sentencing, Griffin was incarcerated in the Omaha Correctional Center. When I looked up his prison photo in 2011, he was wearing a gray sweatshirt with a white t-shirt underneath. He had a moustache and goatee, a receding hairline. I read that his alias name was Poppa Bear. He wasn't smiling, of course, but something about the eyes was different than what I expected. He looked wary. Even, perhaps, frightened. I'd heard what happens to child molesters and rapists in jail, and maybe that had happened to him. Joe N. Griffin was not the scary guy I remembered. I might pass him on the street without a second look. The prison record said that he was scheduled for release in March 2013.

•

The first time I remember encountering danger was on the Miller and Paine escalator, when I was three years old. Riding between the first and second floors, I'd squeezed my fingers around the rubber belt of the hand-rail and, suddenly, got my thumb stuck inside the belt. I tried to pull free, with no success. "Ow," I said. My mother looked down, saw what had happened, and began tugging frantically at my hand.

We glided toward the second floor. The handrail belt crawled into a dark hole. I stared at the hole. I wasn't scared, particularly, but rather more curious about what would happen next.

I'd been unaware, of course, of the story of my life that lay ahead, oblivious to the existence of the Shipping and Receiving department in the basement of Miller's where a certain boy would work years later, who would cross the lawn at a party in 1981 and introduce himself as Prince Charming, and, after a brief summer romance, disappear from my life for close to thirty years.

And then he came back. What is gone sometimes returns.

In the summer of 2011, this boy and I arranged to meet up again in Lincoln. He lived in Phoenix; I was in North Carolina. When he'd sent me an email in April, I didn't recognize the name in the email address, but by the time I'd finished the message—where he mentioned sitting in my car the night we'd met—I remembered exactly who he was: Prince Charming! Within a couple of weeks, we were sending four or five long messages a day. And then we were both back in Lincoln on a warm evening in June, walking toward each other across my parents' lawn, right next to the driveway where we'd sat in my MG in July 1981.

•

Prince was convinced we'd encountered each other before the night he'd introduced himself when I was standing next to the keg in the backyard of the house at 40th and South. Well, of course he'd seen me at parties on J Street; in fact, he said, at a party there the weekend before the night we met, he'd watched me walk out the door.

But no, he meant before that.

We went back over our shared past in Lincoln. We'd both gone to the ELO concert at Pershing Auditorium in February 1977. Maybe we'd run across each other there? It was possible. And further back: he talked about shopping downtown with his mother and grandmother, buying clothes in JC Penney's, stopping for lunch in the Gold's cafeteria. For him, always a hot beef sandwich, a dish of chocolate pudding for dessert.

We went to Gold's sometimes, I said. But Gold's wasn't as clear to me, as deeply imprinted, as Miller and Paine. I told him about how I could spend whole afternoons in the store, wandering through each floor, sitting on the back stairs between the elevators and the candy department, reading a book I'd gotten from the library down the street and waiting for my mother to get off work.

Would anyone do that now, treat a department store as if it were an extension of her own home?

He'd worked at Miller and Paine in the late 1970s, in Shipping and Receiving. He'd pushed one of those giant carts constructed of heavy cream-colored canvas that had become streaked and stained through the various departments to collect merchandise to be delivered out to the Gateway store.

Maybe we'd seen each other in Miller's. Had he been the boy who'd pushed the cart through the bridal department the day I'd tried on the wedding dress?

Maybe. But he was convinced we'd seen each other even before that. He described an episode when he was a kid, six or seven or eight, downtown with his mother and grandmother. They were walking past Miller's on 13th Street, heading north. He was wearing a yellow shirt he didn't like. He saw, walking toward him, a little girl. She was between two women, and each woman held one of her hands. She was wearing a navy plaid dress and a hat. He and the little girl made eye contact as they approached, and then, after they'd passed, they turned and looked at each other.

That must have been you, he said.

It was odd that this little girl was wearing what sounded like the very dress that I'd modeled at Hovland Swanson when I was four; of course I hadn't worn it outside the store—and I couldn't imagine what other woman, besides my mother, would have been holding my hand. Still, it made a nice kind of sense, that we'd seen each other as children, that we'd kept running into each other as we grew up together in this town that seemed, after all, comfortably small, as if the city itself was playing a sort of match-maker, as if we were fated to be together.

We'd been born at the same hospital, eighteen months apart. Maybe I'd laid in the same crib in the hospital nursery where he'd been a year and a half earlier.

Maybe, I said.

There was no way to know for sure if this actually happened. There was no way to know that it actually hadn't.

•

We drove by the house where his grandparents had lived on Park Avenue, past buildings—now vacant—that had been drugstores and bakeries he'd gone to when he was younger. We drove past the house on J Street, where he'd lived the summer we met. We drove past my old house on California Court, past the beautiful house on the corner of Sheridan Boulevard and Bradfield that I'd coveted ever since second grade.

He understood why I'd coveted it. He understood what the house itself meant. He understood exactly who I was.

He asked me to marry him. I said yes. I thought it might be funny, or fitting, to wear the dress my mother had worn at her own wedding back in 1960, the beige raw silk cocktail dress that she'd bought at Gold's for $32.95.

We decided we'd move to back to Lincoln and we bought a house five blocks from my parents and three blocks from the house where we'd met in 1981. At a yard sale, Prince found a poster advertising REM's appearance at the Drumstick on May 28, 1982. At another sale, he found a book that explained the mystery of the Nebraska state capitol as the Seventh Wonder of the World: The book was called *Architectural Wonders of the World,* and the capitol was listed as number four on the list of the fifty *architectural* wonders. It came in ahead of the Parthenon (number 7). When I explained this all to my father, who was genuinely shocked to learn that the capitol wasn't one of the official Seven Wonders (he'd managed to believe this non-fact longer than I had), he said, "Of course it was ahead of the Parthenon."

•

My friend Tekla, who told me about victim mentality, is a Lincoln native, but she's a few years younger than I am, and she went to Lincoln High, so we didn't become acquainted until we both ended up teaching at the same college in North Carolina. After we'd talked for awhile, it seemed strange that we hadn't met earlier—she was English major when I was in graduate school, both of us taking classes in Andrews Hall, and she'd been good friends with (and often visited) the woman who lived directly behind my house on California Court. Her stepfather worked at the Department of Roads, the same place as my own father. She knew the mean boys from Elliott—because they'd all ended up at the same high school—and when I said, "I wonder what they're doing now," she replied, "oh, they're probably in jail."

As it turns out, Hobart spent six years in prison, from 1980 to 1986, convicted of first-degree sexual assault.

•

Joe N. Griffin was released from custody on August 1, 2013. The Nebraska Sex Offender Registry lists his new address: he'd moved to Lincoln and was living in an apartment approximately three miles from our house.

Outraged, I think, How *dare* he? Lincoln is *my* town.

The week after his release, I drive down the busy street that borders his apartment complex. Why am I doing this? Ever since I found out his address—45th and Holdrege, on the north side of town near the University's East Campus, where the law school is located—I've felt an overwhelming compulsion to see where he lives. I know there's an element of the irrational involved. In fact, I know wanting to see where he lives is something I'd have trouble explaining, so I don't tell anyone what I'm planning to do. I'm not stupid, of course. I won't walk past; I'll drive by in my car in broad daylight. The car's doors are locked. I'm wearing sunglasses.

It's a Wednesday, late afternoon. Three men loiter around the steps that lead from the apartment to the sidewalk in the vaguely threatening way that would make me cross the street rather than walk past them. One stands, facing the apartment; one sits on the top step, facing the sidewalk; and the third sits on a middle step with his head against the stair railing. His back is toward the street, so I can't see his face. But somehow, in that moment I glance over, enough details transmit themselves into my brain—weight, race, age—to trigger the understanding that it's Joe N. Griffin.

I feel the same sensation I had at the lineup, twenty-seven years ago, the physical response of recognition and fear. My fingers tighten on the steering wheel. The man sitting on the top step looks right at me; I look away and the rush-hour traffic pulls me along.

•

In my house on the south side of town, I go to the same grocery store where I used to buy my cigarettes and dog food for Missy after I'd moved back to Lincoln for grad school. Sometimes I run into one of Prince's roommates from J Street there, who owns a house a few blocks away from us. I meet up with my high school girlfriends, and we walk along Sheridan Boulevard, remarking on enviable landscaping arrangements and the rare unfortunate choice of paint color on trim. We refer to this activity as "taking inspiration and passing judgment."

I monitor Joe N. Griffin's whereabouts from my computer. He moves to another apartment on Holdrege; and then his location crosses O Street, to an address near the grade school where the mean boys pushed me down on the playground.

I don't like the fact he appears to be moving south, getting closer.

A low-level anxiety begins to permeate my life. For decades, Joe N. Griffin and the assault in Omaha had been like the knife I'd found in the UN-L parking lot the month after Candice Harms had disappeared. Once I found a place to put the knife, I could forget about it. When Joe N. Griffin was incarcerated, he was contained. I could forget about his existence; the rape receded into the past. But now he's out. He's in my city. Outside after dark with the dogs, I listen for any suspicious sound, imagine possible scenarios—he could walk between the houses, open the gate—but I'd hear that, the dogs would bark. I wonder if I should buy a gun. Inside, I bump into furniture, so distracted by this anxiety that I'm not paying attention to my surroundings.

In 2011, it was Joe N. Griffin's imminent release that caused me to begin examining the past and attempting to make sense of the connections I sensed, intuitively, between the vanishing department stores, the disappearance of Candice Harms, and my own experience with sexual violence. Now, his presence in Lincoln eliminates the reticence I'd maintained about the assault. In fact, I find myself talking about the situation too much, to Prince, to my girlfriends. I keep repeating how I have no reason to be afraid, that there's no way the rapist would come after me, that surely he doesn't even remember my name. I'm conscious of how much I'm rationalizing, how much I'm trying to convince myself of a story I don't quite believe. *Should* I get a gun? Another dog, a Rottweiler or chow? Should Prince and I move up our wedding date so I can take his last name and disguise my identity in that way?

How much am I willing to change?

How much I was willing to change was a subject I used to think about. I'd consciously refused, back in 1985, to let the assault turn me into a different person: I was not going to become someone who focused on her own victimhood, who used words like *rape survivor*, who was afraid of sex. In 1985, I'd made a choice to not let the rapist influence the decisions I made.

And I realize that Joe N. Griffin's presence in Lincoln is altering the way I think. Instead of my usual perspective, the consciousness of the past and the subtext below the surface of the city, I am focused on a potentially dangerous future, on unpleasant possibilities that are likely not to happen. Being mindful that danger exists in the world—even here, in Lincoln—is one thing; letting the thought of danger infiltrate most waking moments is turning me into a different person.

And so I decide to stop dwelling on the subject. I will not let his presence in my town consume my life. I don't return to the victim mentality where I believed myself to be invulnerable to harm, of course; I don't wander around my safe neighborhood after dark, and I make sure the doors are locked before we turn in for the night. I take sensible steps to maintain my safety. But I stop considering the gun, the additional dog, the name change. I don't let my thoughts slide down the slippery slope of disaster when I'm in the backyard after dark.

And then, in November 2014, Joe N. Griffin moves again: out of town, to the Norfolk Regional Center, a 120-bed sex offender treatment center. He is over a hundred miles away, in custody again. Around this same time, the Omaha *World Herald* publishes the results of a study reporters had performed on prisoner release dates, and the article reveals that prisoners were being given too much credit for good time. The attorneys responsible for the erroneous calculations resign. Some prisoners who'd been released too early are rounded up to serve the remainder of their sentences. This might have been what happened to Joe N. Griffin. Or he might have committed another crime and been locked up again. In any case, he's off the streets, in custody, and his incarceration in a distant town seems like a gift from the universe.

•

A few months before our wedding in April 2014, Prince is looking through an architectural antique store and finds an old light fixture that had once hung above the escalators in Miller and Paine. He installs it above the kitchen table. I look at the little piece of the beloved store every day now, one of the very lights that had illuminated the path my mother and I had ascended the afternoon when I was three years old. All those years ago, on the escalator, with my thumb stuck under the belt, I watched the handrail disappearing into the dark hole at the top of the first floor. I wore a coat, so it must've been fall or winter. We might have been in Miller's that day to visit the fabric department, a huge hushed room on the fifth floor that smelled of cloth.

The hole at the end of the escalator was coming closer. My mother continued tugging, both frantic and gentle; she didn't want to hurt me. I wasn't scared, though I probably should have been. "Jesus," my mother hissed under her breath. It was a word she used only when she was truly exasperated. I held still and waited. Seconds before we arrived at the second floor, my thumb came free, and I was safe.

Afterword :: All the Others

Over the years I've wondered what happened to Tara and Diane, to the rest of Joe N. Griffin's victims, to nameless rape victims whose stories I can never know, and to others whose stories have become well known, some all too tragically. Some are well known because, like Alice Sebold, they could tell their stories so powerfully. When I read Sebold's *Lucky* in 2002, many similarities of her experience hit home (the need to maintain a kind of stoicism; the consciousness of other people's responses to the situation; the resistance toward the rape-crisis-center perspective). But the differences did, too. Maybe I owe it to the family I was born into, or to the sometimes too-naïve sense of good fortune that before and mostly since I

haven't been able to shed, though I try to temper my sense of it with caution. Perhaps the years between 1981 and 1985 made a critical difference
in attitudes toward women and their reports of sexual assault. Perhaps it
was the difference in geography, Syracuse versus Omaha/Lincoln. I just
know I'm grateful that my experience didn't derail me any more than it
has. I'm grateful to Sebold not only for her own story but the other tragic
stories she shared, and the way she teaches how important it is to talk
about them, to share them, and then to save yourself.

What is Gone is Texas Tech University Press's
second Judith Keeling Book.

The Judith Keeling Book, established in recognition of a lifetime of achievement
in and dedication to scholarly publishing, honors books that are undertaken
through careful research and assiduous attention to detail, that investigate
questions posed by any inquiring mind, and that make a valuable,
perhaps otherwise unnoticed, contribution to the scholarly community
and to the literary culture of Texas and the American West.

JK

About the Author

Amy Knox Brown is Program Director and an Associate Professor of English at the College of Saint Mary in Omaha, Nebraska. She has been widely published in the *American Literary Review*, the *Iron Horse Literary Review*, *Two Rivers Review*, *Shenandoah*, and the *Virginia Quarterly Review*, among others. She lives in Lincoln.